Distributing Leadership for
Personalizing Learning

Distributing Leadership for Personalizing Learning

Ron Ritchie
and Ruth Deakin Crick

network
continuum

Continuum International Publishing Group
Network Continuum
The Tower Building   80 Maiden Lane, Suite 704
11 York Road   New York, NY 10038
London
SE1 7NX

www.networkcontinuum.co.uk
www.continuumbooks.com

British Library Cataloguing-in-Publication Data
A catalogue record for this book is available from the British Library.

ISBN: 1855394421 (paperback)

Typeset by Free Range Book Design & Production Limited
Printed and bound in Great Britain by Ashford Colour Press Ltd.

Contents

Contents

Acknowledgements

Writing this book has been a learning journey for the two of us. We have valued the conversations we have had with each other and with many others from whom we have learned about learning and leadership throughout our professional lives. During the process of writing the book, which started with an underdeveloped idea about the relationship between personalizing learning and distributed leadership, we have co-generated new understandings about ideas and practices, in both learning and leadership, throughout the process of discussion and writing.

We would like to thank those talented and committed teachers and learners with whom we have worked during the writing of this book and on the projects, research and development that informed it, especially those featured in the case studies.

We would like to thank Tim Small for his contribution, particularly to Chapter 5.

We acknowledge the contribution of others to our thinking, but take full responsibility for the final project. It is a work in progress and, as education continues to transform through increasing personalization, we intend to continue learning about what it involves and how that transformation can be supported.

We could not have written this book without the ongoing support of those close to us including Jill, Tim, Anna, Kate, Lucy, Daniel, Oliver and Jack.

Ron Ritchie and Ruth Deakin Crick
Bristol, March 2007

Chapter 1

Introduction

Context

Education in England is changing dramatically and this book seeks to explore some of those changes that will, potentially, redraw the education landscape over the next few years. At the heart of the espoused national vision for the future is the idea of personalized teaching and learning, articulated by the 2020 Review Group, chaired by Christine Gilbert (2006).

Over the last five years the concept of personalized learning has entered the discourse of professional educators in the UK at all levels, although it has remained, to some extent, an undefined concept and one interpreted by teachers and other educationalists in a variety of ways. It is, however, reflected in policies designed to localize power and choice in the provision of schooling – such as specialist schools, trust schools and academies – and it is the overarching concept which shapes the national strategies that form the framework for what goes on within schools. Personalizing learning is seen as the way to enable system-wide change to improve pupils' achievements and well-being. It also reflects wider changes in society towards more personalization of services. It is the current 'big idea' for school education in England and one that, we believe, does have the potential to enhance and enrich the education experience of future generations of young people.

Personalizing learning is a response to a number of drivers including: an increasingly ethnically and socially diverse society; the knowledge economy; new technologies; new demands with regard to employability; demographic changes; and sustainability with regard to communities and the environment. It is, in our view, a route to sustainable improvement in schools. It requires headteachers, teachers and others working in schools to move away from seeing pupils as 'SAT sitters' who enhance or reduce the school's reputation when results and league tables are published to seeing them as rounded unique human beings.

Personalizing learning and building learning capacity

Essentially, personalized learning, or personalizing learning as we prefer to describe it, is an ideology that inspires an education service to meet the diverse needs of individuals and groups, rather than operating a 'one size fits all' model of provision. According to Gilbert (2006: 5), it challenges education services to take a responsive approach and be 'designed around the needs of each child'. Personalizing learning is described by Hargreaves (2004) as the driver which moves us from a nineteenth-century 'educational imaginary' to a twenty-first century 'educational imaginary' – from the unquestioned assumptions about the social and moral order of education which underpinned modernity to a changing set of social and moral assumptions which are more suited to the globalized, information age of postmodernity. This is a movement from a Fordist metaphor of knowledge production to an ecological metaphor of sustainable learning.

According to Hargreaves (2004: 31), a twenty-first century imaginary has the following characteristics:

- Students' identities and destinations are fluid.

- Intelligence is multidimensional, plastic and learnable.

- Schools are culturally heterogeneous.

- Schools are highly diverse and not interchangeable.

- Schools are designed and organized to provide personalized education for all students.

- Education is lifelong for every student and covers informal as well as formal learning.

- Education is unconstrained by time and place.

- Roles are blurred and overlapping – teachers learn as well as teach; students mentor other students.

- Schools and educators are embedded in complex, interconnected networks; education is user-led.

It is within the context of change implied in this new imaginary that we seek to explore the nature of personalizing learning and how it can be realized in schools and other educational settings. We argue that personalizing learning is essentially about building learners' capacity to learn as they become more aware of their own learning power and progressively take responsibility for their own unique learning journeys.

Personalized learning is sometimes referred to as the 'new progressivism', or a swing back to the more child-centred ideologies of the 1960s and 1970s where the focus was on the *person* who was learning and his/her experience, in contrast to the *knowledge* he or she was acquiring. This sort of thinking sets up *knowledge* in opposition to the *person*. In practice, a knowledge-centred classroom would sometimes function at the expense of some individuals who did not 'fit' and a 'child-centred' classroom would sometimes function at the expense of the rigour and quality of the knowledge that was acquired.

We suggest that the current discourse of personalizing learning allows for a more integral vision of education than those represented by the exhausted language of rigid oppositions between the academic and the vocational, the universal and the contextual, knowledge and the learner. At its heart, personalizing learning represents an ideological shift in power from 'provision' to 'dynamic process'. The focus is on the 'person as a learner in relation' and his or her unique and localized pathway from personal experience and meaning making, to an encounter with the cultural, technological and scientific wealth of what is already known and to the generation of new knowledge.

The aim of personalizing learning is to assist the learner (child or adult) to develop a realistic sense of self, or personhood, while going about the task of developing a personal portfolio of qualities and competencies that will enable them to respond to the material condition of humanity and survive in the world as it now is. It aims to shift the focus away from knowledge as a commodity towards the processes and narratives that can carry the intention of the learner in their quest for meaning and value, and to reconcile a personal, dynamic and unpredictable approach to learning with the rigorous and specialized norms of a knowledge-based curriculum and its assessment and accountability framework.

Personalization represents a paradigm shift in which learners are empowered to participate in their own processes and pathways of learning, through choice and self-evaluation. Such a paradigm shift is a move towards a profoundly different value system and a redistribution of power. The purpose of this book is to explore the implications of this redistribution of power for school leadership or, to put it another way, to explore what sort of leadership is optimal for the creation of learning communities in which student self-evaluation, participation and choice in learning becomes a reality.

Leadership and building leadership capacity

The current context for schools in England is undeniably one that has become increasingly complex over the last few years. In particular, policy initiatives such as the requirements of *Every Child Matters* (DfES 2003) and the *Children Act* (DfES 2004), together with the drive to more personalized learning mean that schools face an ongoing period of change (NCSL 2005a). These changes require those working in schools to take a much broader view of the needs of young people and recognize, for example, the need for much more inter-professional collaboration if the five outcomes of the *Every Child Matters* agenda (be healthy, be safe, enjoy and achieve, make a positive contribution and achieve economic well-being) are to be addressed. Indeed, West-Burnham (2005: 30) argues that, 'The introduction of personalising learning represents a leadership challenge of a significantly different order of magnitude to those which have dominated school leadership in recent years. A substantial proportion of the reforms have been top down strategies based on improving schools. There is no hegemony for personalising learning.'

It is widely recognized that leadership of schools is crucial to the successful implementation of change and school improvement. The significant role of headteachers has been well researched and documented. Ofsted inspections and the Chief Inspectors' annual reports have provided ample evidence of the part headteachers play in effective schools (Ofsted 2006). It is difficult to conceive of a school that is successful in the current climate that is not well led.

However, Ofsted and others have, for some time, recognized that leadership by an individual leader, however committed and hard working, is unlikely to be adequate. Schools are increasingly dealing with a diverse range of policy initiatives that have made it difficult for headteachers to take individual responsibility for leading all developments, even if they so desired. In the words of Ofsted (2003: 35), 'It is no longer true – if it ever was – that leadership and management are the sole responsibility of the headteacher. High-quality leadership and management must now be developed throughout a school's organisation if these new challenges, many of which require working much more closely in partnership with other schools and agencies at all levels, are to be met successfully.'

Consequently, distributed leadership, that is learning centred, is becoming increasingly common. This involves more holistic approaches in which the combined strengths and enthusiasms of a broader group of staff are actively involved in the leadership of developments focused on improving the learning and well-being of young people. It is not a single approach but a way of viewing leadership that recognizes the hidden capacity for leadership that exists in schools and needs releasing and nurturing. It is about distributing expertise and experience for the benefit of all. Distributed leadership implies a focus on leadership at all levels of the school community, not merely designated leaders. Indeed, we regard young people as also having the potential to contribute to the leadership capacity of the school. However, distributed leadership without effective internal accountability within the school is not going to be the driver for the improvement we advocate. Distributed leadership requires staff and students to become mutually accountable within the values framework of the school.

Linking personalizing learning and distributed leadership

It is our claim, based on evidence offered in this book, that building leadership capacity within schools through distributing leadership is conducive to personalizing learning for young people and the school improvement that results from this.

Like personalizing learning, distributed leadership is about the personal, not merely about structures and organizations. Both learning and leadership (and we argue that they are inextricably linked journeys) are about personal growth and 'becoming'. For that reason, the book uses the metaphor of a journey to characterize processes by which emergent learners become effective lifelong learners and emergent leaders become effective leaders. These journeys are unique for individuals and understanding them requires an understanding of the learning selves involved. They are journeys that take place in social contexts and collaboration between teachers and between pupils, teachers and other adults, including parents, are as essential to personalizing learning as they are to distributed leadership.

Further chapters

Chapter 2 focuses on the nature of learning in the context of the information age. It explores frameworks for personalizing learning. We introduce the idea of the ecology of personalization, and discuss the gateways that might be involved (adapted from Hargreaves 2004). These suggest a deep and transformative pedagogy rather than simply a focus on techniques or strategies. We have combined the gateways into the following four 'deeps': deep learning (assessment for learning, student voice, learning how to learn); deep experience (new technologies, curriculum); deep support (mentoring and coaching, advice and guidance, personalizing teaching); deep leadership (design and organization, workforce reform, distributed and learning-centred leadership). This chapter emphasizes the person as a learner, the notion of the learning self and the dimensions of learning power (Deakin Crick 2006), which are revisited at several points in the book. These dimensions are: changing and learning; critical curiosity; meaning making; creativity; learning relationships; strategic awareness; and resilience. Learning is described as a process of becoming an intentional learner who knows him or herself as a learner and is able to progressively take responsibility for his or her own learning journey. It is a process through which learners become increasingly interdependent and responsible for themselves. We explore learning pathways that might be followed to achieve a range of personalized learning outcomes. The chapter concludes with a consideration of the nature of learning relationships and issues related to power.

In Chapter 3, we look at the significance of leadership for personalizing learning in schools. We begin with a general exploration of leadership before discussing the nature of distributed leadership, stressing that this is not a single phenomenon but a complex reconceptualization of leadership and how leadership capacity can be built in schools. It is an approach that extends the boundaries of leadership and, indeed, focuses on leadership as a concept that is broader and more appropriate than the notion of key or designated leaders. We address the nature of learning-centred leadership which puts the learning of all (adults and young people) at the heart of the leadership endeavour. The need for those contributing to leadership to be effective learners is explored. We emphasize, again, the importance of relationships to learning, in this case, through collaboration and teamwork among professionals. The chapter outlines the research into distributed leadership and identifies factors in schools that are conducive to it becoming embedded. These include the qualities needed by the headteacher as symbolic or designated leader in the context of distributed leadership.

The core idea of the book is amplified in Chapter 4. We examine the parallels and links between personalizing learning and distributed leadership. We further develop the idea of learning and leading as journeys with a direction and moral purpose and show the deep interconnectedness between the two. Effective leadership is necessary to create conditions for effective learning and being an effective learner is essential to becoming an effective leader or someone effectively contributing to the school's leadership. Leadership involves learning and supports learning. We propose four learning stations on these journeys: the learning self; personal qualities, values, attitudes and dispositions for learning; publicly required and personally valued competencies; and the acquisition of publicly assessed and valued knowledge and know-how. The centrality of relationships is reinforced in this chapter – they are essential to learning and leadership.

The following three chapters look at the themes of the book in the context of headteachers, middle leaders and teachers. We gave serious thought to the order of these chapters; beginning, as we do, with headteachers is not intended to reinforce hierarchical models of leadership. Indeed, in the spirit of distributing leadership, prioritizing the leadership capacity of teachers has a logic. However we decided, in recognition of the role of headteachers in facilitating distributed leadership, we should start with their contribution to personalizing learning through distributed leadership.

Therefore, headteachers, as the formally designated leaders of schools, are the topic of Chapter 5. We discuss the role of the headteacher in enabling distributed leadership and in empowering others to contribute to the leadership capacity of the school. Headteachers are the key agents to building their own leadership capacity and the leadership capacity of the school. The chapter considers headteachers' learning journeys, their learning selves and their identities as learners. We highlight the importance of the role models headteachers provide for others in the school (adults and young people). Headteachers are often resolving dilemmas and holding what we describe as creative tensions between, for example: providing flexibility and acknowledging constraints; making innovations and avoiding risks; thinking longer term and delivering short-term results; and encouraging teamwork and assessing individuals. The qualities of effective heads are discussed and the nature of professional relationships that heads form and sustain are discussed in the context of school ethos and culture. Headteachers, we suggest, improve the quality of learning and teaching in schools through their influence on staff motivation, commitment and environment. We return to the gateways to personalizing learning and analyse the headteachers' role as gatekeepers and agents of change. This chapter includes case studies from primary and secondary schools.

Chapter 6 focuses on middle leadership and those with formally designated leadership titles and roles. The structure of this chapter parallels that of Chapter 5. We locate this discussion in the context of national standards for subject leaders and guidance, although we emphasize the development of middle leaders' capacity as stories of personal growth in the social context of schools with appropriate cultures and ethos. The significance of middle leaders' authenticity as leaders, if they are to influence colleagues, is emphasized. The chapter discusses the challenges that subject leaders, as middle leaders, face in schools seeking to personalize learning for young people. The chapter again features both primary and secondary case studies. The primary one illustrates the contribution of a science subject leader and the support provided by her headteacher. The secondary case study features the work of an English teacher who was responsible for Key Stage 3 English in a school in very challenging circumstances.

The third chapter in this section of the book looks at the role of teachers and pupils as leaders of learning. It recognizes the need for individuals to take responsibility for their own learning journeys. The section on learning selves tackles issues related to choice and voice. The chapter also addresses the theme of 'leading and following'. It examines the learning self of the teacher and the pathways that they might take. The professional relationships that teachers form with their pupils and with each other are explored, as is the role of the teacher as a learning guide who scaffolds the learning of others. The case study in this chapter is an example of a primary teacher's work in collaboration with teachers from other local schools. The project described involved the development of learning and teaching strategies within a curriculum resource based on Brunel that used the seven dimensions of learning power to foster personalized learning and learning how to learn.

The final chapter brings together some of the overarching themes of the book. The challenge for leaders is to create the optimum conditions for learning, change and growth for all members of the learning community. This chapter identifies some of the creative tensions that operate in the sort of 'relational and ecological' paradigm that supports the distribution of leadership and personalization. It explores some of the core values that underpin such a culture and identifies some of the implications for leadership development for individuals, organizations and for the system as a whole.

Conclusion

Paradigm shifts are, to some extent, impossible to recognize as they are happening. In the examples in this book we illustrate schools and classrooms that are in the process of transformation rather than at a point where we could, with any confidence, claim they provide evidence of the shift that is implied by personalizing learning. It will be a few years before such examples are available but we hope this book will be supportive of the process of change. We invite you to use our text, which grew out of our learning conversations, to stimulate new discussions about the implications for your own settings and practices. Much of the agenda for personalizing learning sounds straightforward but the reality of embedding such principles and practice as, for example, assessment for learning is challenging. The challenge is of course increased in the current context of accountability (with the related bureaucracy), intensification (as, for example, extended schools increase workload and, potentially, stress) and what some regard as the commodification of education.

Therefore, the improvement of young people's educational experience through increased personalization will only happen and make the impact we aspire to if these concepts are owned locally and reconstructed to meet local needs and within local contexts. There is no blueprint for personalizing learning. That is the challenge for the future and we wish those of you directly involved in schools success in this important endeavour.

Chapter 2

What is personalizing learning?

Introduction

In this chapter we explore the impact of the information age on the processes of learning and achievement. We map out the general terrain and key themes of personalizing learning, and then explore how these cohere in a complex ecology. We then explore particular themes of the person, the processes, the relationships, the pathways and the outcomes of learning. As we do this, we begin to identify key themes which have to do with power, direction and relationships – and thus with leadership.

Changing worlds: learning in the post-mechanical age

The impacts of technological innovations, globalization, the universal accessibility of knowledge, cyber culture, political, cultural and ideological diversity and the knowledge economy are well discussed and form the background for the discourse of educational innovation and change, including that of personalized learning. What is less well explored, however, is the impact of these things upon human beings: their relationships with the material and social world and the competencies they need to survive in it. The new technologies are built on a network logic that provides an immensely flexible structure to support innovation and growth – enabling much of what is known to be taken apart and reconstituted almost instantaneously to suit a new question, hypothesis or analytical purpose. It is no longer the sorting and storing of existing knowledge that is required of new knowledge workers but know-how and the ability to relate and harness knowledge to identity and purpose, by personalizing, adding value and meaning, re-designing and re-presenting what is known in a new context. These are the ways in which an individual can get a purchase on the complex networks that shape his/her world and are shaped by his/her response.

In search of the self

Harnessing knowledge and learning to identity and purpose is a key element of personalization. The relationship between the local and the global has changed – there is a gap between the experience, the lived reality of students' lives, and the ways in which knowledge, relationships and values are encountered in the abstract, virtual and global ether. A young person's experience of the material world is formed very significantly through cyber space – heroes, news, relationships, entertainment, friendships, knowledge – can all be technologically mediated. Students rarely belong simply to a homogenous, local, geographical community with its particular stories, traditions, rituals and funds of knowledge – they belong to multiple, diverse and often virtual communities, frequently with 'interrupted stories' and traditions as a result of migration, and changes in the social fabric of society.

In search of a sustainable social world

In this context, it is important to reformulate the ways in which learning and the formation of identities and relationships work together in the development of active learner/citizens. MacBeath and colleagues (2004) use the term 'learning in the wild' to describe learning that is embedded in relationships; centres on the needs of learners; supports the development of skills and dispositions and crosses age and institutional boundaries. The implication of such learning is that we need to attend to the person as much as the process and outcomes and we need to do this in a manner that integrates personal and social development with learning and achievement. This is a key challenge for personalizing learning.

Frameworks for personalizing learning

In a key text which summarizes 42 theoretical frameworks for thinking and learning that have been used since the Second World War, Mosely and colleagues (2005) identified seven of these that they describe as 'all embracing' frameworks that seek to provide a comprehensive account of how people learn and think in a range of contexts, rather than just deal with one aspect of learning, such as cognition. What is common to these seven is that they treat the learner as a 'whole person', who thinks, feels, hopes and has a sense of self as 'chooser' or agent in his or her own learning journey. They all, to some degree, see the learner as a person in relation to other people, capable of communicating and collaborating with co-learners, and learning from experience. They acknowledge that the learner is 'embodied', although they do not explicitly look at the location of the learner in a particular community, with its own social practices, traditions and world views.

Mosely and his colleagues (2005) go on to identify the principles used in all 42 of the frameworks they examined in their handbook. These are:

Domain:

- area of experience
- subject area.

Content:

- types of objective
- types of product (including knowledge product).

Process:

- steps/phases in a sequence or cycle
- complexity
- level in a hierarchy
- type of thinking or learning
- quality of thought or action.

Psychological aspects:

- stage of development
- structural features of cognition
- nature and strength of dispositions
- internalization of learning
- orchestration and control of thinking
- degree of learner autonomy
- level of consciousness.

This summary of research maps out the sorts of principles that are relevant to learning, and to personalizing learning. Most of the contemporary learning theories and practices with which we are familiar will fit into this framework, and we will mention three of them in particular – multiple intelligence theory, emotional intelligence and spiritual intelligence. What is less clear in this set of principles is the nature and role of relationships in learning. We think that this is an important area that has had less attention than it deserves, and we will explore it in more depth later.

Multiple intelligences

Gardner's theory of multiple intelligences (1983) was a major challenge to the classical view of intelligence as a single unitary capacity, which was genetically determined and easily measured by an IQ test. He developed a theory of the mind as a 'series of relatively separate faculties with only loose and non-predictable relations with one another' (1983: 83). These have become known and widely utilized by teachers as a means of recognizing and accounting for the reality of children learning in multiple ways and having differing strengths and weaknesses. Teachers who want to attend to the whole child as a learner find Gardner's theory helpful because it draws attention to the different needs of learners and the different ways in which children learn. Although there is little empirical evidence to support this theory, it has a very significant theoretical and scholarly foundation. There are eight intelligences which, Gardner argues, represent a full account of human cognition:

1. Linguistic intelligence
2. Logical-mathematical intelligence

3. Musical intelligence

4. Bodily-kinesthetic intelligence

5. Spatial intelligence

6. Interpersonal intelligence

7. Intrapersonal intelligence

8. Naturalistic intelligence.

Emotional intelligence

Emotional intelligence is closely linked to Gardner's interpersonal and intrapersonal intelligences. There is a significant body of professional knowledge and research which focuses specifically on this human capacity to recognize and understand one's emotions, and the emotions of others, and to respond to that knowledge in a manner which shapes action and facilitates growth and learning. Hadden et al. (2005) argue that emotional literacy is a potential in everyone that is contingent on the interaction between a person and their social context, rather than a capacity that is either present or absent in the individual.

Understanding and managing one's feelings and emotions are important for learning. We know less about this, but there is evidence that 'good thinking' requires 'good feeling'. Hauenstein (1998) argues that teachers should treat learners as whole people and his theory attends equally to the development of feelings, values and beliefs as to gaining knowledge. He says that all learning involves feeling and doing as well as thinking, and that the aims of education should be to help students 'develop their critical, reflective and problem solving abilities and skills in all three domains' (1998: 29). His levels of development in the affective (emotional) domain include:

- receiving
- responding
- valuing
- believing
- behaving.

As well as being relevant for the individual learner, emotional literacy is important for the learning community. Hadden et al. (ibid.) developed a CORE framework for emotional intelligence in school that has three components: communication, organizational factors and relationships.

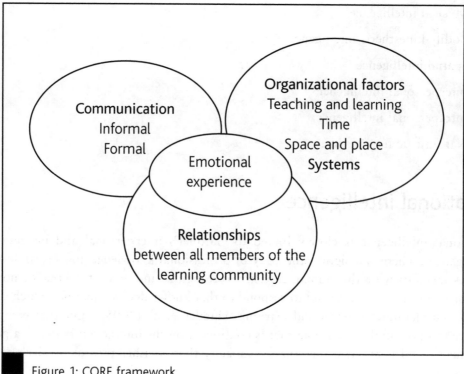

Figure 1: CORE framework

They show that the emotional literacy of the school is influenced by:

- the quality of relationships between all members of the learning community
- the way in which time and space is used to organize activities
- the nature of communication about core processes.

In particular, their theory shows that the nature and quality of teaching and learning are crucial to students' perceptions of their school as an emotionally literate place – in other words, for students to feel 'it's OK for me to be here'.

Spiritual intelligence

Spiritual intelligence is a less well-developed concept and one that can be challenging in practice. The growing interest in spirituality in education has been described by Wright (2000) as a 'spiritual renaissance' stimulated by the advent of postmodernity and its rejection of 'pseudo-rationalistic' dogma. He says, 'Spirituality is an elusive and dynamic concept whose complexity is revealed when viewed in the light of: a mind-matter dualism; the contrast between the sacred and the profane; and the notion of spirituality as the cultivation of self-awareness. Despite their differences, these three routes have in common a concern for the ultimate meaning, purpose and truth of human existence. (2000: 14)'

In relation to learning, spirituality has to do with 'meaning making' and 'learning that matters to me', as well as a personal and social commitment to truth seeking. It relates to purpose and motivation – if what teachers want students to learn has no personal meaning to them, there will not be much learning taking place. In a study of over 500 16–19 year olds in one city, Arthur and colleagues (2006) discovered that young people have a robust sense of spirituality, which includes core values of care and justice and a desire to 'become the best person I can'. While they were generally negative about organized religion and politics, they were angered by injustice and engaged in personal spiritual practices. The capacities required for critical spiritual reflection are part of the personal and communal processes of learning. In personalizing learning, the learners' own spirituality matters, and it is equally important that the traditions from which they draw their spiritual resources are seen as a key educational resource rather than something to be left at the door of the classroom.

Three different models of the learner

It is clear from the substantial review of research evidence by Mosely and colleagues that the ways human beings learn and change is a complex and multidimensional phenomenon. It is all too easy to focus on one aspect at the expense of another, and our focus, of course, is profoundly shaped by the world views, values and beliefs that shape how we see the world. Helen Haste (2001) identifies metaphors of the learner representing three major models from psychological research for defining human 'competence' or 'meta-competence'. These are the learner as a:

- puzzle solver
- story teller
- tool user.

The puzzle solver model values individual cognitive functioning, with rational decision making as both a value and an attainable goal. The story teller model understands human beings as meaning making creatures, with narrative, sign, symbol and rhetoric as core features of cultural transmission. The tool user model sees human beings as developing through their interaction with tools (including language), and these tools can change the way they interact with the world. The tool is a prosthesis for the human body and mind, which can transform the way we interact with the world.

The point is, that in addressing personalizing learning, it is important to explore the underlying values and beliefs that shape how we see the world, and to recognize that these will have an impact on the sorts of classrooms and schools that we create and lead, and our understanding of personalization.

Evidence from the classroom and school

So far we have considered research into qualities of human beings that are relevant to personalizing learning. This is only a part of the story, and there is a growing body of research that explores the sorts of practices that teachers who are learner centred will participate in. In a summary of research-informed principles from this programme, Black and colleagues (2006: 9) say, 'A chief goal of teaching and learning should be the promotion of learners' independence and autonomy. This involves acquiring a repertoire of learning strategies and practices, developing positive learning dispositions, and having the will and confidence to become agents in their own learning.'

They identify seven principles that have emerged from several research studies within the Economic and Social Research Council's (ESRC) Teaching and Learning Research Programme, which they suggest may help teachers, leaders and policy makers direct effort and resources to support learning and achievement – or in other words to become learner centred.

Effective teaching and learning:

- equips learners for life in its broadest sense
- engages with valued forms of knowledge
- recognizes the importance of prior experience and learning
- requires the teacher to scaffold learning
- needs assessment to be congruent with learning
- promotes the active engagement of the learner
- fosters both individual and social processes and outcomes.

These principles are 'headlines' for the sorts of social practices that will facilitate sustainable learning.

The ecology of personalization

Personalizing learning cannot be reduced to a single factor – such as class size, or a particular strategy such as assessment for learning. Shaping provision around students' diverse needs requires a culture that is learner centred, and this is best understood through an ecological metaphor, rather than a mechanical one. An ecology suggests that there are a number of variables – for example, in a garden: soil, light, water, heat, seeds... and not least the interventions of the gardener – all of which need to be appropriately balanced and timed for the full growth and flourishing of plant life. A change in the amount of light available will have an impact on everything else; too much water will literally drown the plants and the wrong soil chemistry will reduce growth or accelerate it to the point of collapse.

This concept of personalizing learning through the creation of a particular climate or culture is widely supported. The DfES (2005) identifies five core components of personalized learning: assessment for learning; teaching and learning strategies; curriculum entitlement and choice; school as a learning organization; and external partnerships. The ESRC Teaching and Learning Research Programme have welcomed this and argue that 'deep educational change' will need to ensure that the focus on learners and learning includes learning dispositions and learning identities. James & Pollard (2004) suggest that it is not about 'fitting the individual into the system' in a mechanical fashion, but rather it is about the development of social practices that enable people, as learners, to become all that they are capable of becoming.

For schools as learning communities, there are several entry points into personalizing learning. For school leaders, this means becoming learning centred, by which we mean attending to the social processes and structures that will facilitate learning at all levels of the organization. A school whose organizational values and practices are shaped by learning will create the optimum conditions for personalization. For the learner as story teller and tool user, the learning community, with its particular climate and values expressed in the quality of its relationships, is part of a sensitive ecology which will either support or inhibit learning. This is another relatively under-researched area – that is the ecology of the learning community that creates the greatest synergies for learning and personal development.

Hargreaves (2004) identifies nine gateways that are applicable to every school and classroom. He selected this set because they are familiar to practitioners; they require leadership and promote a focus on learning and achievement. These are:

- curriculum
- assessment for learning
- learning how to learn
- new technologies for learning
- workforce development
- mentoring and coaching
- school design and organization
- student voice
- advice and guidance.

These gateways can be entered by school leaders at a time and place appropriate for a particular school. We suggest that these are gateways to deep and transformative learning – that is learning that takes account of the whole person, their stories, traditions, hopes and aspirations, and supports the learner on a lifelong journey of change, growth and development. As we described in Chapter 1, this means deep learning; deep experience; deep support and deep leadership in a context of deep organizational change that takes account of the complex range of factors that we know influence learning.

Some of the core elements of a learning ecology that we have identified are: the learning self; learning how to learn; competencies for life; a learner-centred curriculum; teacher/learner relationships; learner-centred pedagogy; learning context and community. There is a growing body of evidence that these are deeply related to each other. One of us led a research project with 600 students from the ages of nine to 14 that explored: the relationship between students' 'learning power'; their perceptions of their teachers' learner-centred practices; their achievements in the National Curriculum Assessments; and their sense of their school as an emotionally literate place. The findings suggest a positive association between all of these things (Deakin Crick et al. 2007a). The findings concluded that:

Distributing Leadership for Personalizing Learning

- Learner-centred teachers are those who:
  - create positive interpersonal relationships with students
  - stimulate higher-order thinking
  - honour student voice
  - cater for students as individuals.

- When students perceive their teachers to be learner centred they see themselves as able to learn and change. They report higher levels of critical curiosity, meaning making and creativity, and they are more strategically aware of themselves as learners and have healthier learning relationships. In short, they have more learning power.

- Where the opposite is the case, students are more fragile and dependent as learners.

- Learner-centred teachers, and students with high levels of learning power also perceive their schools to be 'emotionally literate' places – that is a school that enables members of its community to interact in a way that builds understanding of their own and others' emotions, which can then be used to shape their actions.

- Students with the most learner-centred teachers had the highest levels of motivation, learning power and feelings of emotional safety in school.

- Students in groups that were highest in learner centredness and emotional literacy tended to have the highest levels of attainment as well as higher levels of learning power.

- There is evidence of a positive relationship between students' learning power and their attainment, although there is some conflict between the more active aspects of learning power and conventional assessment practices.

- Students who have higher levels of strategic awareness and creativity are likely to have higher all-round learning power profiles.

- Teachers who are highly controlling in their teaching style are likely to produce classes with lower levels of attainment and learning power.

Further studies have shown a relationship between underachievement and students' learning power and early research data suggests a relationship between students' behaviour and their learning power profiles (Leo et al. forthcoming 2007).

It is clear from this summary so far that personalizing learning is a complex phenomenon, in which the learner is part of a particular, intentional community of learning, which itself is located in a wider political, social and cultural context. The relationship of this to the practice of leadership is also complex – and it is the theme of this book that leadership can manifest in individuals at all levels in the learning community and in a variety of ways. The term 'education' derives from the Latin 'educare', to lead out. To the extent that we understand personalizing learning through the metaphor of a dynamic journey over time, undertaken by the learning community, then concepts of changing and learning, or movement from one state into another, go hand in hand with the concept of leadership, vision and direction setting. Leadership, to some degree, can be shared by all members of the learning community.

24

In order to develop these links we will go further into an exploration of the person, the processes, the relationships, the pathways and the outcomes of learning. We will do this with particular reference to concepts that are relevant to leadership and personalization.

The person: the learning self

In the frameworks for learning that we have discussed so far, it is all too easy to forget that at the heart of it all is a person, with a particular story to tell, likes and dislikes, dispositions, struggles and hopes. Furthermore, that person is nested in a set of relationships and a particular economic and social setting with its own traditions, rituals and funds of experience and knowledge. When the learner comes into the classroom, all of these factors come too!

When we think about the learner as a whole person, then it is clear that the concept of learning identity is important. A learning identity is 'a sense of myself as a learner'. Take a few minutes to think about yourself as a learner, and try writing some answers to the following questions:

- 'I am the sort of learner who chooses to...'
- 'I am the sort of learner who tends to...'
- 'I am the sort of learner who prefers...'
- 'I am the sort of learner who dislikes...'
- 'I used to be the sort of learner who...'
- 'I am becoming the sort of learner who...'
- 'I am the sort of learner who believes...'

These are the sorts of questions that are deeply personal and your answers are probably unique (unless you read them from a textbook), because each human being has a unique identity. Personalizing learning means that learners are encouraged to:

- become aware of themselves as learners
- take ownership of their unique learning identity
- take responsibility for their own learning process and pathway.

Focusing simply on skills, strategies and processes of thinking and learning does not necessarily attend to the person of the learner, yet the person is at the heart of personalization.

These ideas have been developed through research and practice into learning power. Learning power is described by one of us (Deakin Crick 2006: 5) as 'A form of consciousness characterised by particular dispositions, values and attitudes, expressed through the story of our lives and through the relationships and connections we make with other people and our world.'

To put it another way, learning power seems to be a form of awareness about oneself as a learner. It can be recognized in particular behaviours, beliefs and feelings about oneself and about learning. It finds expression in particular relationships, where trust, affirmation and challenge are present and it is 'storied' in the memories a person brings to their learning and in their future hopes and aspirations.

Our research identified seven dimensions of learning power, which are a mixture of values, attitudes and dispositions, that can explain and inform learning behaviour. These are:

Dimensions of learning power	What this dimension means	What I think and feel and do in this dimension
Changing and learning	A sense of changing and growing as a learner.	I know that learning is learnable. I know that my mind can get bigger and stronger just as my body can. I feel good about my capacity to learn. I expect to change as time goes by. I celebrate my learning.
Critical curiosity	An inclination to ask questions, get below the surface of things and come to my own conclusions.	I want to delve deeper and to find out what is going on. I don't accept things at face value. I want to know how, why, what and where. I don't accept information without questioning it for myself. I enjoy finding things out.
Meaning making	Making learning personally meaningful by making connections between what is learned and what is already known.	I like to fit new bits of information together with things I already know. I like to make connections between subjects. I love learning about what really matters to me. I draw on my own story in my learning as well as the stories of my community. I learn at home, in my community and at school.

Dimensions of learning power	What this dimension means	What I think and feel and do in this dimension
Creativity	Risk taking, playfulness, lateral thinking and using imagination and intuition in learning.	I like to play with ideas and possibilities. I trust my intuition and follow my hunches. I use my imagination in learning. I like to be challenged and stretched.
Learning relationships	The ability to learn with and from other people and to learn on my own.	I like sharing my thoughts and ideas with people. I like learning on my own as well. I learn from adults and people at home. I like learning with and from other people. I know how to help others learn.
Strategic awareness	Being aware of, and actively reflecting on and managing my own learning feelings, processes and strategies.	I know how I learn. I can manage my feelings of learning. I plan my learning carefully. I think about thinking and learning. I am aware of myself as a learner – I know what I like and dislike. I can estimate how long tasks will take.
Resilience	The tenacity to persist in the face of confusion, not knowing and failure.	I know that making mistakes is a natural part of learning. I am not afraid of having a go. I tend to keep going at a task until it is completed. I don't fall apart when I fail. I keep going at my own pace – I know I will get there in the end. I know that struggling is an important part of learning.

Figure 2: Seven dimensions of learning power (Deakin Crick 2006: 8)

Strategic awareness

Perhaps the most crucial element in building learning power is the capacity of the individual to become strategically aware of themselves as a learner. Within this learning power dimension is the notion of reflectively aware learners, able to recognize and take responsibility for managing their own feelings, thoughts and processes in relation to learning.

The purpose of strategic awareness is the development of learners' independence and autonomy that James and Pollard (2006) argue is one of the chief goals of teaching and learning. These terms perhaps fit best with the metaphor of the learner as a 'problem solver', an individual, rational being. However, if we work with the metaphor of the learner as a 'story teller' or 'tool user' we might prefer to say that the purpose of developing strategic awareness is the development of 'intentional' learning (Black et al. 2006). This implies a sense of agency, choice, intention and desire – there is a person who has an intention and a desire to learn something, but he or she is not necessarily an isolated, autonomous individual, rather someone who takes responsibility for their own process and pathways of learning. We prefer the term 'responsible learners' to 'independent or autonomous learners' – suggesting that learners can take responsibility for themselves as learners and they are embedded in particular local and global communities which have an impact on how and what they learn.

Self-regulation

Self-regulation is understood by some (Zimmerman 2000; Demetriou 2000) and by ourselves as including, but not limited to, metacognition, which Flavell (1976: 232) described thus: 'Metacognition refers to one's knowledge concerning one's own cognitive processes and products or anything related to them.'

Demetriou in particular not only sees self-regulation as the overarching concept that includes metacognition but also the conscious control of motivational, affective and behavioural processes. So self-regulation, thinking about thinking, managing one's own interests and aspirations and managing the feelings and processes of learning are all important processes that develop the learning self. Developing the intention to learn means finding the will and motivation to learn, as well as managing the process.

Motivation for learning

Of all the concepts about the learning self, motivation is perhaps the most complex. What makes one person want to learn one thing and another learn something else is influenced by a range of factors, both internal to the learner and in the learner's environment. The American Psychological Association's (1997) *Fourteen Learner Centered Principles* include three that directly address motivation. These are:

- Motivational and emotional influences which are affected by the learner's emotional state, beliefs, interests, goals and habits of thinking.

- The learner's creativity and curiosity that contribute to intrinsic motivation to learn.

- The effect of motivation on extended learner effort and guided practice.

McCombs and Whisler (1997) identify self-awareness and beliefs about personal control, competence and ability, clarity and salience of personal values, interests and goals, expectations of success and failure, and general states of mind as central factors.

The will to learn is derived from a person's sense of deep meaning or purpose and is directly related to the amount of effort they are willing to expend on a task. What is relevant here is that without a sense of meaning and purpose, there is not likely to be much learning. The dimension of 'meaning making' in learning power refers, among other things, to 'learning that matters to me' or learning that 'connects with my story'. Human beings are meaning making creatures, and when the content of what students are required to learn is meaningless to them, or is meaningful only because it represents an external reward, then there is less likely to be deep learning taking place. Making sense of what is being learned, connecting it with what is already known and experienced as well as with a sense of direction in learning and desire is a crucial self-process that cannot be ignored.

An important element of strengthening and supporting the learning self is 'student voice'. Deep listening and responding to what the learner has to say about herself, her experience and desires, is perhaps the most crucial means of affirming the 'selfhood' of another. Rudduck's (2004) research into pupil consultation for improving teaching and learning demonstrated that the impact of listening to students and including them as fully active participants and co-researchers in learning was significant and included greater engagement, a more positive learning environment, improved learning, improved student self-esteem and better learning relationships.

Learning processes

If 'becoming an intentional learner' is the overarching goal of teaching and learning, the practices that teachers engage in to support learning can be evaluated against this goal. McCombs' work into the assessment of teachers' learner-centred practices identified four factors that contributed the most to student motivation for learning and achievement. Interestingly, the key predictor was how the students perceived their teacher to be doing on four themes:

- How well the teacher is able to create positive interpersonal relationships.

- How well the teacher is able to 'honour student voice'.

- How well the teacher is able to stimulate higher-order thinking.

- How well the teacher is able to cater for individual differences.

Three of these factors have to do with the quality of relationships and one of them relates to the specific skills and strategies for learning how to learn and achievement (McCombs 1997). We will look specifically at relationships later. Of all of the practices that teachers engage in, assessment is perhaps the single most powerful tool. Tools can be used for good or ill, and we know from substantial research evidence that an over focus on summative testing and assessment – that is testing for grading and labelling purposes – actually depresses motivation for learning (Harlen and Deakin Crick 2003a). The challenge is to develop assessment practices that support learning, and are personalized to particular learners.

The Assessment Reform Group (2002) says, 'Assessment for learning is the processes of seeking and interpreting evidence for use by learners and their teachers to decide where the learners are in their learning and decide where they need to go and how to get there.' They go on to say that assessment for learning should be part of core school and classroom planning, that it fosters motivation, that it is about equipping learners to take responsibility for their own learning and that it supports achievement.

Assessment, that supports learning and learning how to learn, is a key process that involves both the learner and the teacher in a dynamic movement between the learner and the 'text' of the curriculum. We use the terms 'curriculum' and 'text' here to mean the formal funds of knowledge, skills and understanding that are publicly valued, that constitute the content of what is learned. The teacher is a guide or a mentor to the learner, selectively directing attention between the self and the text, in a dynamic and bespoke process, in which power is progressively given to the learner. Assessment data is used formatively by the teacher to support the learner in knowing what to do next and how to achieve a particular learning goal.

This process of support is sometimes called 'scaffolding'. A scaffold is used to support a building until the building is strong enough to support itself. The scaffolding processes of learning involve the teacher as a guide and leader of learning and the learner as an active agent. The scaffolding zone is the relationship between them as they attend dynamically to both the learning self and the 'text' of the desired learning outcome.

For example, waiting several seconds for students to answer a question stretches the scaffolding zone, while the learner utilizes his or her learning power for the shared purpose of understanding something. Research showed that the average wait time in questioning in a particular study was desperately short – the teacher's attention would be focused on the text rather than the self of the learner (Tobin 1987).

Another example would be the use of mind maps as a means of organizing thinking and learning around a particular topic. The process of constructing a mind map is a sort of scaffold for the learner's thoughts and ideas, helping him or her to connect concepts and link things together. It is also a means for the teacher to understand what is happening for the learner – sharing 'what's inside their head' by putting it on paper.

Learning pathways

However, it is not just about the person and the process. There are funds of knowledge that learners need to acquire. In the classroom there are schemes of work, and recognized sets of knowledge, skills and understanding that are important both for their own sake and for their application in future employment niches. The acquisition of these set pieces is judged by an assessment system that publicly formalizes the outcome – people with a set of qualifications.

We are not saying that these qualifications are not important – but the pathway of the learner from personal choice and meaning making to meeting the formal requirements of the curriculum is part of the ecology of personalization. It is common educational practice that the acquisition of knowledge is top down – beginning with the big themes dictated by the formal content of the curriculum, such as 'rivers' in geography, rather than personal experience, such as 'a particular, local and personally chosen and experienced river'. There is not often the opportunity for students to make meaningful choices about what they learn or how they learn it. The same technologies that create the need for personalization also make it worse through assisting the subjection of human beings and what they know to measurement and fragmentation – whether this is through timetables, risk assessments, bytes, performance management, hedge funds, digital timing/dating – and significantly for schooling, an overwhelming focus on high stakes, summative assessments.

One of the key principles in all of the frameworks for learning identified by Mosely and colleagues (2005) was the notion of sequencing in the complex process of learning and acquiring knowledge. Different steps in the process involve different levels of learning and types and qualities of thought and action.

A pathway that begins with a personal choice on the part of the learner and ends up with a formal assessment of a recognized body of knowledge may involve not only the acquisition of a particular body of knowledge or set of skills, but it may also entail the formation and development of the learner's identity and selfhood, through personal meaning making and the process of reflection.

The following eight steps have been developed in an RSA project that explored how learning power and a personalized approach to a competency-based curriculum might work together (Deakin Crick et al. 2007b).

First, the student is encouraged to choose an object or place that fascinates them. Careful, hands off prompting and guidance may be needed from the teacher, to ensure that personal interest is strong and authentic. The rest of the process will be highly influenced by the integrity of this choosing process. (Sometimes the 'object' turns out to be a person, or event – it is its susceptibility to observation and the strength of the student's interest and engagement that are important.)

Second, they observe and analyse the chosen object/place, both as a separate, objective entity and in relation to their own interest and reasons for choosing it. In this, they are developing their sense of personal responsibility. This initiates the cycles of a personal development process that is recorded in a workbook and in which the student, tutor and later others participate. It requires the student to develop the critical curiosity and strategic awareness necessary for independent learning, in the context of effective learning relationships. Students are also developing a sense of themselves as learners who can change and grow over time.

Third, the student starts asking questions. They should be obvious but open ones, such as: How did it get there? What was there before? Why is it how it is? Who uses it? How and why did they get involved? The student is initiating and conducting a process of enquiry and investigation, driven by personal interest and shaped in turn by the answers to their own questions. They are exercising and developing critical curiosity. (All the time, the student is encouraged to reflect on their motivation, reasoning and identity as a motivator of their own learning.)

Fourth, the questioning leads to a sense of narrative, both around the chosen object and in the unfolding of new learning. Historical and present realities lead to a sense of 'what might be' both for the object/place and for the learner and their learning. They are becoming the author of their own 'learning story' or journey.

Fifth, the learner begins to discern that this ad hoc, subjective narrative leads in turn to new, objective facts and knowledge. Subjective learning starts to be related to a wider, objective awareness. The learning becomes a knowledge map that can be used to make sense of the journey and of new learning as it comes into view. The student is making meaning by connecting new learning to the story so far.

Sixth, with informed guidance and support from the teacher, the student's widening map of knowledge can be related to existing maps or models of the world: scientific, historical, social, psychological, theological, philosophical and so on. This is where awareness of the diversity of possible avenues of learning becomes useful. It requires the teacher to act as supporter, encourager and tour guide in the student's encounter with established and specialist sources and forms of knowledge.

Seventh, the student arrives at the interface between their personal enquiry and the specialist requirements of a curriculum, course, examination or accreditation. Their development as a learner enables them to encounter specialist knowledge and make sense of it, in relation to what they already know and in the way they already learn, interrogating it and interacting with it, instead of simply receiving it, using the model of learning and knowledge-mapping skills they have developed through the enquiry. This is where the resilience will be tested, which will have started to grow through the responsibility and challenge of a self-motivated enquiry.

Eighth and last, the student can forge links between what they now know and institutional and social structures receptive to it: qualifications, job opportunities, learning opportunities, needs, initiatives, outlets, relationships, accreditation, publication and so on. Initially, this takes the form of a portfolio or presentation, based on the workbook, making explicit both process and outcomes of the enquiry. The student's learning has met its communicative purpose. They have created a pathway from subjective response and observation towards the interface with established knowledge. In doing so, they have also achieved life-enhancing personal development by asking and answering such questions such as: Who am I? What is my pathway? How did I get there? Where does it lead me? What were the alternatives? Who helped me and how?

The progressively more demanding, spiral sequence of thinking and learning processes involved in these eight steps are:

- choosing/deciding
- observing/describing
- wondering/interrogating
- discovering/storying
- navigating/mapping
- spanning/connecting
- interacting/incorporating
- reconciling, validating.

Integrated curriculum

This eight step process is one that may fit within a particular topic, or scheme of work, but in this case the learner's choice will be somewhat bounded. To fully utilize these ideas, particularly supporting the learning self, a school needs to re-frame the curriculum from one that is tightly framed by subjects to one that includes an integrated approach to knowledge. Many schools are developing approaches to the curriculum that are organized around a set of core competencies, and thus have a more integrated and learner-centred approach to the learner's pathway through the content of the curriculum. A competency is a 'whole person' response to a complex demand – the RSA's Opening Minds curriculum identifies competencies for learning; managing information; managing situations; relating to people and citizenship. This has been developed significantly at St John's School and Community College in Marlborough, Wiltshire, where many of the ideas we are describing in this book have also been explored through research and development projects (see Bosher and Hazlewood 2005).

Personalized learning outcomes

What are the implications of personalization for learning outcomes? It has already become clearer that personalization is likely to lead to a range of types of outcomes that are, in some way, distinctly relevant to the learner. Learning outcomes can be personal, social, academic and vocational (and more). For example, for some learners at some stages, simply learning how to choose and decide may be a perfect outcome (it is surprising how little choice our students actually have in their learning as they go through school). For others a publicly validated mathematics or science qualification might be a perfect outcome. In the first case, the learners themselves have the authority to validate and evaluate, and this can be supported by the teacher. In the second the mathematics or science community has the authority to validate and evaluate. What makes them both personalized is the meaning they have to the learners and the learner's ownership and understanding of and participation in the personal learning journey that led to the particular outcome, and its relevance in their life narrative.

Learning relationships for personalization

All teachers and learners know that the quality of relationships between teachers and learners is a crucial component for learning and achievement. In a 'one size fits all' model of education, with Fordist timetabling and outcomes dictated by the requirements of set examination pieces, the attention and value placed on the quality of relationships can easily fade into the background. In a context of personalization, in which assessment is more like a 'mentored movement of selective attention between self and text' the quality of relationships move to centre stage.

Carl Rogers (1994), the pioneer of humanistic psychotherapy, identified unconditional positive regard, authenticity and empathy as the key elements of the sorts of relationships that will facilitate learning. Our research into learning power suggests that trust, affirmation and challenge are key qualities, and McCombs' work on learner-centred practices shows that it is how the *student* perceives the quality of relationship that really matters.

So teachers and leaders who are able to facilitate learning will be able to be authentic, entering into a relationship with the learner without presenting a front or a façade. The feelings that she (the teacher) is experiencing are available to her, and she has a direct personal encounter with the learner, meeting her on a person-to-person basis. It means that she is being herself. Secondly the learning guide will be able to care for the learner in a non-possessive manner, which accepts the other individual as a person and learner in her own right – a basic trust that the other person is fundamentally trustworthy as well as being an imperfect human being. It means that the teacher is able to empathize with the learner, understanding the learner's reactions from the inside – including the nature of their thinking as well as their emotional orientations and needs.

The skill of the teacher/learner relationship is in the manner in which the teacher can build on this basic trust and stretch the students' learning power by challenging them to progressively higher-order creative and critical thinking, to becoming intentional learners and to extending their knowledge, skills and understanding.

In our learning power research we use the term 'learning zone' to capture the idea that the learner can enter a particular space or mindset as a whole thinking-feeling-reflecting-acting person, and they can be invited to enter that space with their teacher. We also use metaphors of animals or cartoon characters, such as *The Simpsons*, to carry the ideas. For example, when someone is learning how to choose, they can enter the 'springboard zone' (creativity) with Bart Simpson, and do 'idea spinning', until they learn to identify what they, personally, are interested in. While in this zone, they are stretching their creativity 'muscles' and their learning power dimension. The teacher is scaffolding this process and it depends crucially on the quality of trust, affirmation and challenge in that space.

The implications of this for leadership are that personal and interpersonal qualities of the teacher as leader are really important. How a leader is able to balance between nurture and structure in their care of others, between their own authentic feelings and their capacity for 'here and now' whilst taking account of situations, is as important a professional quality for a leader of learning as it is for a psychotherapist. Modelling and imitation are basic ways in which human beings learn and form their identities. 'Mimetic desire' is about wanting what someone else has – and we all tend to imitate people we admire, for good or ill. As Palmer (1983) says, good teaching is based on the integrity and identity of the teacher. How the teacher is as a learner – and how they model their own learning power – is a professional issue.

For students, personalization also means collaboration, by which we mean learning from and with other people. Apart from being a necessary skill for life and for citizenship, if learning and leadership are distributed and the focus is on the process as much as the product, then students can learn huge amounts from each other through modelling and imitation and through coaching. Students are often able to understand each other in ways that are inaccessible to the teacher and can therefore support and scaffold each other's learning in a way that builds community and decentres the teacher – and frees the teacher's time.

Another, more subtle, aspect of learning relationships relates to the fact that in students' lives, their immediate and extended family, and their community and tradition form part of the relational network which provides resources for their learning. We know some students coming from dysfunctional and deprived families are deeply disadvantaged in their heritage of learning relationships. Less well understood, though, is the concept of middle-class deprivation in which young people have impoverished local communities and traditions on which to draw. Latchkey kids, nurtured by children's television, geographically separated from extended families, and without access to community-based activities, may lack the social and cultural resources, including shared stories, values and traditions which enrich and support learning.

Linked to this is the importance of celebrating diversity in learning relationships and resources, as it is expressed in different cultural and religious traditions. The meta stories of particular religious and cultural traditions in the communities in which students find themselves are designed to be transmitted from one generation to the next. Critically engaging with these communities and their traditions is a powerful part of the personalization of learning – and indeed of citizenship education.

Personalizing learning, power and leadership

We have explored a range of themes and principles which we believe are part of the ecology of personalizing learning. At heart, it is about attending to the person who is learning and to the learning community in a manner that enables learners to take responsibility for their own learning over their lifespan. We have looked at how some of the elements of personalizing learning fit together and we have focused particularly on the person, the processes, the pathways, the outcomes and the relationships of learning.

Personalizing learning is challenging precisely because it means a shift in power, a 'letting go' of control, from the teacher as the repository of knowledge to the learner as author and agent of his or her own learning journey. This needs to happen in a way that respects and does justice to the learning of others, including the learning of others over history that has contributed to the funds of knowledge that we are introducing our learners to. This directly links with our theme of leadership, since leadership is about the power and authority to lead a community in a particular strategic direction, through particular personal qualities, capacities and skills. How and where leadership operates in schools will have a direct impact on the degree of personalization of learning that is possible.

Chapter 3

The nature and benefits of distributing leadership

Introduction

The previous chapter has indicated the challenges of introducing or developing approaches that personalize young people's learning. This chapter explores the implications of these challenges for school leadership and seeks to outline a distributed approach to leadership which, we will argue, is particularly conducive to school improvement that focuses on personalizing learning. If personalizing learning is the goal, we see distributing leadership as the means, or engine, for getting there.

As we explained in the first chapter, the current context for schools in England is one that is both complex and challenging. Agendas, such as those mentioned in Chapter 1, including *Every Child Matters* (DfES 2003) and the *Children Act* (DfES 2004), when added to the aspiration of personalizing learning, mean that the job of headteachers (and teachers) has never been harder.

In order to meet those challenges, we argue that leadership needs reconceptualizing. We need to move away from the model of a single leader to a more inclusive approach that views the leadership capacity of the school as something that involves all staff, and as something that can be increased over time. Leadership capacity, like learning power, needs to be built and that process needs facilitating. Leadership is, therefore, not just about doing, it is as much about the potential for doing and how that can be released. It is about synergy and the fluid relationships between leading, following and context. We seek to reinforce the idea that leadership is a more powerful and inclusive concept than leaders, particularly of the 'heroic' type. Leadership is also a more complex concept and building leadership capacity through distributing leadership is no easy option. It is significantly more difficult and complex than the appointment of a designated leader.

This chapter begins with a general exploration of the nature of leadership before considering what is meant by 'distributed leadership'. We go on to emphasize the need for all those contributing to a school's leadership capacity to see themselves as learners in learning-centred schools – where the learning of all (pupils and adults) is recognized as essential to school improvement. We discuss factors that are conducive to distributed leadership in schools, including the need for collaborative cultures that foster teamwork.

Like West-Burnham (2004), we see leadership as 'rooted in personal authenticity' and that authenticity is 'the interaction of values, language and the capacity to act'. Building leadership capacity takes time and support. It involves the personal growth of those involved as they become effective in their leadership roles.

What is leadership?

Before exploring distributed leadership, it is necessary to clarify what we see as key aspects of leadership more generally.

There is sometimes confusion between leaders and managers as opposed to leadership and management. West-Burnham (1996: 54) provides a very useful illustration that emphasizes the importance of a leader when he says, 'Imagine a long and complex journey. It is the role of the leaders to secure agreement on the destination, to ensure that the purpose of the journey is kept firmly in mind and provide guidance and support. Managers ensure that all the resources are available in the right place at the right time, sort out any detours and obstructions and ensure that timetables are adhered to. Administrators keep track of the fuel consumption, check that appropriate documentation is available and ensure that managers and leaders can do their job. All three functions are essential but without leadership the journey is, literally, pointless.'

Although leadership and management are interdependent, our emphasis in this book focuses on the importance of leadership.

Leadership is about vision, often through co-constructing a view of a preferred future in collaboration with others and building on shared values. It is therefore about bringing about change for improvement. It embraces a moral dimension – it is the means by which an institution lives out its values better in practice and, within that, individuals do the same. It is about co-constructing, communicating and sharing a vision. It is about strategic planning to enable the preferred future(s) to be realized in a purposeful way. The best way to achieve a preferred future is to construct it, not to wait for it to happen as a result of the work of others. Leadership is about professional relationships that facilitate change and improvement. It is about empowering others to engage them in the realization of improvements. It involves mutual accountability through ongoing monitoring and evaluation to check progress and modify practices as necessary. It involves working creatively to make effective decisions and solve problems in order to achieve the agreed goals. To quote from *All Our Futures* (NACCCE/DfEE 1999: 102), 'Outstanding headteachers are creative, risk-takers. They value and use creativity in their own thinking, in management, in teaching and learning and in the curriculum. They hold fast to their conviction that creativity in all its forms must significantly affect the children and teachers in their schools and their futures.'

Leadership is a complex concept and takes many different forms depending on the individual concerned and/or the context in which it occurs. Bush and Glover (2003) provide a useful typology of leadership that reminds us of the complexity and different perspectives. These include:

- Instructional leadership: 'The critical focus for attention by leaders is the behaviour of teachers as they engage in activities directly affecting the growth of students' (Leithwood et al. 1999: 8).

- Transformational leadership: Building a unified common interest between leaders and followers (Gunter 2001) involving: building a school vision; establishing school goals; providing intellectual stimulation; offering individualized support; modelling best practices and important organization values; demanding high performance expectations; creating a productive school culture; and developing structures to foster participation in school decisions (Leithwood 1994).

- Moral leadership: Focusing on values and the ethical stance of leaders. Fullan (2003) refers to the 'moral imperative' of leadership, by which he means the responsibility all leaders should take for the learning of students in their own institution and beyond it.

- Participative leadership: Focusing on the decision-making processes of the group and teamwork.

- Managerial leadership: Emphasizing the importance of the managerial dimension of leadership.

- Postmodern leadership: Recognizing the diverse and individual perspectives of stakeholders.

- Interpersonal leadership: Focusing on collaboration.

- Contingent leadership: Recognizing the need to adapt leadership styles to particular situations.

Bush and Glover (2003) recognize these are somewhat artificial distinctions and that 'successful leaders' are likely to embody most or all of these approaches.

Another commonly used framework for leadership is that related to leadership styles proposed by Hay McBer (NAHT 2001: 11) which includes the following styles: authoritative; coercive; democratic; pacesetting; affiliative; coaching. Examples of these modes and styles of leadership are given in later case studies.

Effective leadership is essential to the successful implementation of any change, especially something as complex as the implementation of personalized learning. Leadbeater (2005) quotes Derek Wise, headteacher at Cramlington School, who, he says, summed up the approach of the leaders they encountered in their research on personalizing learning. Wise states, 'We are not just interested in doing a little better with the current system. We are interested in transformation. We want to do something radically different because that's the only way to have a big impact.'

According to Leadbeater (2005: 9), 'Leaders sanction a culture of innovation so that staff – and pupils – can devise better approaches to learning...The heads in these schools are not heroic leaders. Their leadership style is often understated. They focus on drawing out contributions from others, rather than thrusting themselves into the limelight. They are the antithesis of the "super-head". They do not compromise on a floor of high standards but they also believe learning must be motivated by a compelling goal.'

These are leaders then who recognize the need to disperse or distribute leadership so that the institution benefits from the collective leadership capacity of all involved. Inevitably, the nature of that involvement will vary and for some teachers, especially at the beginning of their careers, it will be through being effective classroom teachers, developing their leadership of a class. Our premise is that the potential of everyone in a school to develop and contribute leadership qualities needs to be recognized and fulfilled. The task of a headteacher is to release the potential leadership capacity of others in the school.

What is distributed leadership?

Clearly, distributed leadership is not a single phenomenon. It is a somewhat contested label for a range of approaches that has attracted attention for a number of years in education (Bennett et al. 2003a; Gronn 2002a; MacBeath et al. 2004).

Bennett et al. (2003a) conducted a systematic review of literature that related to distributed, democratic, dispersed and distributed leadership and found little agreement as to the meaning of the term. They identified 'a number of different interpretations of leadership which shared some characteristics that could be drawn together into a possible understanding of the term'. They suggest that, 'It is best to think of distributed leadership not simply as another technique or practice of leadership but, just as importantly, as a way of thinking about leadership. If we understand it in this way, it challenges many current assumptions about the nature of leadership and the community within which it occurs.'

Bennett et al. go on to say that 'distributed leadership is not something "done" by an individual "to" others, or a set of individual actions through which people contribute to a group or organisation'. Gronn (2002a) suggested distributed leadership is 'an emergent property of a group or network of individuals, in which group members "pool" their expertise'. Consequently, distributed leadership involves people working together in a 'concerted way' such that 'the amount of energy created is greater than the sum of the individual actions'. Distributed leadership is a group activity that works through and within relationships, rather than individual action. It is an approach that does not restrict leadership opportunities and challenges to teachers. It can apply equally to other adults who work in schools – especially significant in the context of workforce reform and new policy directions (such as *Every Child Matters*), which are leading to an expanding range of professionals working in schools to support young people. Distributed leadership can emerge from a variety of sources depending on the issue and who has the relevant expertise or creativity.

Bennett et al. (2003a: 3) suggest that distributed leadership will involve many more people than might traditionally be assumed: 'The group within which the "concerted" leadership action develops should not be limited to a small number of people with formal senior roles. The writing we reviewed raised the question of the "boundaries of leadership", i.e. which individuals or groups should be involved in leadership activity within an organisation or section of it, and gave no clear answer to the question. However, it clearly called into question the traditional attachment of leadership roles exclusively to posts such as head of department or assistant headteacher.'

Distributed leadership is not equivalent to delegation from one individual to another. Harris (2004) distinguishes distributed leadership by highlighting that it involves:

- distribution of responsibility (which Harris equates with power)
- working through teams (not just individuals)
- engendering collective responsibility.

Distributed leadership is best thought of as invitational rather than imposed. Effective headteachers invite and open doors to others to take on leadership opportunities, regardless of title and status. The rewards are often, therefore, in terms of job satisfaction and professional fulfilment rather than financial gain. It should be, we consider, an entitlement with which comes responsibilities to act with a moral imperative. Such approaches to leadership have a strong democratic dimension (Woods 2005).

The National College for School Leadership currently promotes distributed leadership as a preferred mode of leadership. It takes the view that the distinctiveness of 'distributed' is that it separates leadership from leadership roles and titles and challenges traditional structures and organization (NCSL 2004a: 3). They identify 'Five Pillars' of distributed leadership in schools:

- self-confident and self-effacing headship
- clarity of structure and accountability
- investment in leadership capability
- a culture of trust
- a turning point.

NCSL (ibid.) recognizes that distributed leadership refers both to what people do and the organizational conditions in which they do it. Distributed leadership means more than leaders and leadership in schools and refers, as well, to 'the conditions in which people exercise leadership – the organization and culture, and the inter-relationships that enable leadership at every level to be exercised in line with the school's strategy and purpose'.

To put it another way, distributed leadership has both agential and structural dimensions and, in order to understand what distributed leadership entails, it is important to understand the interplay between these two dimensions (Woods et al. 2004).

A further element of distributed leadership's distinctiveness is reciprocal interdependency – 'where one leader's practice becomes the basis for another leader's practice and vice versa' (Spillane et al. 2003: 344). This involves understanding leadership as the 'circulation of initiative' in which the individual initiates action and change, within the resources and constraints of their organizational context and, through this, contributes to the flow of activity and the shaping of that same organizational context (Woods 2004). Distributed leadership is not a set of simple features but represents a complex mix of structural, cultural, social and individual characteristics and actions.

Crucially then, distributed leadership:

- extends the boundaries of leadership
- challenges traditional hierarchies

- is an holistic approach using the combined strengths and enthusiasms of staff
- involves purposeful action of professionals working together collaboratively
- can emerge from a variety of sources depending on the issue and who has the relevant expertise or creativity
- encourages autonomy and interdependence with effective internal accountability.

In schools, we see examples of distributed leadership where individuals (with or without formal leadership titles) are given opportunities to lead: a project or initiative (such as to introduce assessment for learning); a team or enquiry group (perhaps investigating the impact of strategies for personalizing learning); staff development or training (related to such strategies); a whole-school dimension or theme; a subject or group of subjects.

Understanding distributed leadership also requires us to explore issues related to hierarchy, autonomy and sources of change in schools.

All schools, apart from perhaps Steiner schools, involve hierarchical organizational structures. All have a headteacher, or equivalent, and most have a designated deputy or assistant heads and other tiers of staff with differing responsibilities. Distributed leadership involves approaches that, in effect, work across or outside such organizational structures and allow colleagues to work in teams that involve participants from different levels in the institution working together as equal partners. The leadership of such teams, as we will see through later case studies, does not always involve colleagues with a leadership title.

Organizations also involve degrees of control and autonomy within their operation. West-Burnham and Coates (2005) see control as associated with low trust and dependency. They argue a continuum from control, through delegation and empowerment to subsidiarity (a balance between shared consent about certain overarching principles and local autonomy), which they see as involving high trust and interdependence.

Where aspects of distributed leadership are evident, the staff did, in one of our experiences, consider themselves to have a significant degree of autonomy (Ritchie 2004; 2007a). Such autonomy fosters a sense of ownership and engagement in developments. It can encourage lateral and creative thinking and risk taking if individuals do not feel themselves to be heavily controlled or 'micro-managed'. This autonomy may be within a self-monitored or negotiated values framework (hence the subsidiarity referred to above). An example would be where the school vision or mission is shared and explicit and staff operate semi-autonomously within that framework and with effective systems of monitoring and internal accountability. In this way, distributed leadership is not an invitation from a school leader for a free-for-all in which anything goes. However, it does involve trust. Individuals need to feel – and be – trusted by the school leader if they are to have the opportunity to take risks as they introduce new developments.

It is our premise, shared by others (Hargreaves 2004), that the development of personalized learning requires strong leadership that is likely to be of a distributed nature if it is to succeed.

What is 'learning-centred leadership'?

Effective leadership in school should also be learning centred. The term 'learning-centred leadership' comes from another dimension of the work of the National College for School Leadership and draws on the work of Geoff Southworth (2004). Learning-centred leadership places learning 'centre stage' (Sergiovanni 2001) and is characterized by a focus by leaders and those involved in leadership on learning – that of students and of teachers and other adults. Southworth (2004) suggests that learning-centred leadership involves the following dimensions:

- modelling – learners learning from the models of practice provided by others
- monitoring – collecting, analysing and acting on assessment data
- dialogue – fostering learning conversations among teachers and others related to learning and teaching.

The NCSL (2004b) promotes a model of learning-centred leadership where:

- school leadership is committed to individual and organizational learning
- leadership responsibility for learning is explicit
- shared knowledge creation is supported through research and professional development
- leadership is underpinned by systematic management
- a learning culture is promoted where learning is talked about and celebrated.

In the context of personalizing learning, learning-centred leadership has a number of distinctive characteristics according to West-Burnham (2005: 26):

- openness to change
- focus on the individual
- rich dialogues for learning
- modelling strategies to support learning
- high quality personal relationships
- shared knowledge creation
- leadership underpinned by systematic management
- a culture of success.

Learning-centred leadership clearly involves the leadership of the development of personalizing learning if that is accepted as a condition of effective learning by students, as we discussed in Chapter 2. It is not, however, easy, as Dean Fink reminds us: 'Leaders of the 21st century are like the three-legged man, like Jake the Peg. They have one leg in traditional public administration, since most still work in hierarchical bureaucracy; one leg in new public management as they struggle with regular standardised tests and site-placed management; and a third leg in learning communities as they work to refocus their schools and communities on students' learning. The challenge for leaders and education is to learn how to balance all three legs – simultaneously – without falling flat on your face' (Quoted in NCSL 2005b: 21).

Why should leaders regard themselves as learners?

Learning-centred leadership involves a focus on adult learning as well as young people's learning. This highlights another aspect of successful leadership – it involves a commitment to continuing to learn about leadership in order to more effectively support students' learning. A theme running through the case studies found in this book will be the emphasis that individuals involved in leadership activities give to their own learning. That learning may result from ongoing reflective (and sometimes, reflexive) practice (Ghaye and Ghaye 1989; Winter 1998); through informal collaboration and/or dialogue with other professionals; through mentoring and coaching (see www.curee.co.uk for the National Framework for Mentoring and Coaching and Powell et al. 2001); through formal professional development programmes; or through systematic action enquiries (Ritchie and Ikin 2000) and other research activities. Like younger learners, leaders as adult learners need to develop positive learning dispositions and the dimensions of learning power we discussed in Chapter 2, such as creativity, resilience, strategic awareness, apply equally to all learners whether we are talking about a Year 1 child or an experienced headteacher. We will revisit these dispositions in the context of leadership in the next chapter.

Why are collaboration and teamwork important?

Distributed leadership, as noted above, is very much about teams rather than individuals and is based on the belief that working collaboratively has benefits that working alone does not have. Within schools, working collaboratively has become much more the norm than it was a few years ago. Based on Ofsted data, many successful schools have a culture conducive to effective collaboration and teamwork. Leadbeater (2005: 14) notes from his research, 'personalised learning schools have a highly collaborative ethic'.

However, effective collaboration does not merely result from putting individuals together – in the same way that sitting pupils round a table does not, necessarily, lead to effective group-work. Teams often need to be facilitated and the conditions for effective teamwork established. Factors that seem particularly conducive to effective teamwork are trust (Bryk and Schneider 2002) and mutual respect. Structures can be established within a school's organization to support teamwork – for example, by providing formal processes for establishing teams for specific purposes; auditing team skills (through, for example, the use of Belbin's tools – see www.belbin.com) and developing individuals' team skills; and by providing protected time for team discussions.

Educational professionals have also been increasingly encouraged to collaborate and network across schools in order to improve the quality of their work through a variety of national initiatives over the recent past, including:

- Leadership Incentive Grants (LIGs) (see www.standards.dfes.gov.uk)

- Excellence in Cities (EiC) (see www.teachernet.gov.uk)

- Networked Learning Communities (NLCs) (see www.ncsl.org.uk)

- Specialist Schools Network (see www.standards.dfes.gov.uk)

- Leading Edge Partnerships (see www.standards.dfes.gov.uk)

- Federations (see www.standards.dfes.gov.uk)

- Primary National Strategy Learning Networks (see www.standards.dfes.gov.uk).

Additionally, local authorities often promote clusters of schools or schools themselves form self-supporting networks or seek funding (for example, through European funding such as Comenius). It is difficult to believe that these kinds of opportunities for creative collaboration would have been available to or indeed welcomed by the traditional heroic leaders more common in the 1970s, who would tend to run their schools by the singular exercise of power and control. It is also interesting to note how these centrally driven initiatives have altered the delicate balance in the national policy context between competition and collaboration, since the Education Reform Act of 1988 introduced the notion of market forces to the education system.

These initiatives have led local, regional, national and international networks to promote learning. Hargreaves (2004: 13) believes that 'networks of schools and of teachers constitute the infrastructure for innovation and for the transfer of created knowledge and new practices'. He notes that they can be centralized or decentralized; hard (formal) or soft (informal); strong (involving high levels of trust) or weak; open (inclusive) or closed (exclusive). The benefits (and challenges) of networking are well documented (Hopkins and Jackson 2003b; Jackson 2002). Most schools find themselves in more than one network – indeed large secondary schools can be in many.

Hargreaves (2004: 17) argues that school leaders should:

- audit the networks in which a school is involved

- analyse existing networks for fitness for purpose

- assess their benefits and costs

- adjudicate on the priorities

- advocate cross-membership

- adapt through monitoring changes in value.

Networking between schools can provide excellent opportunities for leaders and aspiring leaders to learn more about effective leadership and exchange ideas about effective practice, including strategies that support personalizing learning.

How can leadership capacity be extended within a school?

If the boundaries of leadership are to be extended and the leadership capacity of the organization increased, there is a need for leadership development to be taken seriously and planned (Harris and Lambert 2003).

Research by one of us (Ritchie 2004, 2007a) involved the generation of case studies of schools where distributed leadership was regarded as evident (by local authority officers) and these cases provided insights into the approaches to leadership development used in such schools.

In all cases, there was evidence of the headteachers providing positive role models for teachers as leaders. This provided examples of reciprocal interdependency as discussed above. Numerous examples of headteachers coaching and mentoring colleagues as leaders were found, especially in the primary schools. Robertson (2005) has a full and excellent discussion of the nature and value of coaching. Coaching is, in practice, a means of personalizing leadership development as it tailors the support to the particular needs of the coachee. It is a strategy with particular benefits for the emotional dimension of professional learning (Goleman 2002). Mentoring is, according to West-Burnham and Coates (2005), a strategy that brings together the three strands of learning-centred leadership proposed by Southworth (2004): modelling, monitoring and dialogue. Modelling, where leaders provide positive examples to others, seemed to be a particularly powerful mode to influence and support less experienced colleagues. It can inspire and motivate. Of course, poor role modelling can have the opposite effect and lead to disillusionment and demotivation.

In some cases, headteachers were explicitly challenging teachers and other adults in schools to move out of comfort zones in terms of leadership responsibilities (for example, by encouraging inexperienced teachers or learning supporters to lead particular projects or to cover a maternity leave). In schools where leaders were explicitly seen as learners, their learning was supported through institutional structures such as enquiry groups at a primary school and school-based staff development provided by a senior colleague in a secondary school.

Support for teachers taking on 'acting' roles was evident in several primary schools as a way of developing teachers' and deputy headteachers' leadership capabilities. Early internal promotion was another aspect of leadership development noted, usually associated with additional support from the headteacher. Shadowing or paired subject leadership/SENCO role was also contributing to leadership development, as well as succession planning in several primary schools.

The local authorities' role in leadership development was highlighted in several schools. In some cases this related to centre-based leadership and management courses and initiatives. In other cases it related to local authority-led school-based INSET, while in some cases the support advisory teachers and advisers were providing INSET in schools. Local authority-supported cluster groups were providing valuable opportunities for subject leaders. Other forms of networking were also cited as valuable forms of leadership development (sometimes linked to specific projects). In some schools international experiences were seen as significant in supporting teacher learning about learning and leadership.

Higher education contributed to leadership development in a variety of ways. In several schools, middle leaders were valuing the accredited programmes, such as MAs, they were doing or had done. Other opportunities that teachers had to take on roles beyond their schools were also positively impacting on their professional development related to leadership roles. NCSL programmes were praised in several schools.

What factors are conducive to distributed leadership?

According to the research referred to above (Ritchie 2004; 2007a), schools where distributed leadership is embedded, and therefore sustainable, show evidence of the following factors:

- the school – has explicit values, ethos and aims
- the culture – is collaborative and structures exist to foster collaboration and teamwork.

Staff:

- feel valued, trusted, listened to and well supported by the headteacher
- are involved in creating, sharing and developing a collective vision for the school
- are challenged and motivated
- regard themselves as learners
- are aware of their talents and of their leadership potential
- relish the responsibilities and opportunities that they are given
- feel supported and enabled to take risks
- appreciate the autonomy they are given.

Schools where distributed leadership is embedded are ones where it is accepted by all involved as the preferable mode of operation for the school. There is linguistic alignment in that, for example, a common learning language is used as well as directional alignment in that everyone is working towards the same goals.

They are schools where:

- The hierarchical aspects of organization are played down and minimized.
- Staff consider they have some autonomy and feel empowered.
- The sources of change and development are, at least to some extent, internal to the school (rather than imposed externally through policy requirements) and bottom-up (as opposed to always resulting from the headteacher).

- There are informal and spontaneous opportunities for staff to play a part in leadership, as well as structural means for encouraging this.

The role of the headteacher in encouraging and supporting distributed leadership is another key strand of the research. Factors related to headteachers, associated with embedded distributed leadership, identified through analysis of the data include:

- the head has a clear vision

- the head listens to staff

- the head provides a good role model

- the head is good at identifying and valuing colleagues' strengths

- the head trusts colleagues

- the head is supportive of colleagues.

They are schools that Sergiovanni (2001) describes as 'culturally tight and managerially light'. The headteachers in the cases where leadership is distributed demonstrate many of the characteristics of what Ronnie Woods (2002) calls 'enchanted headteachers'. These include:

- Pride, a selfless pride, a generosity of spirit, a pride in their people and their achievements.

- Closeness to the children and an acute awareness of their needs and where they come from. They believe that their school is making a huge difference to children's lives. They demonstrate a passionate commitment to teaching and learning, to the quality of provision, to maintaining high standards, to developing fully rounded individuals well prepared for the next stage of their lives. They know what is going on, and everyone knows they know.

- Respect for and sensitivity to the needs of others, placing a high value upon quality of relationships throughout the school community. This respect and sensitivity is modelled strongly in all they say and do. They are builders of teams and developers of people.

- An optimistic view of change as challenge – not a blind acceptance of change but a view that the school must keep moving forward, can always improve further. Imposed change is to be taken, adapted and made to work in their schools.

- Good at listening, encouraging the contribution of others, accepting constructive criticism and admitting mistakes. And being self-reflective in doing so.

- Viewing themselves as nothing special. They are acutely conscious that much of what they do and how they do it is context sensitive.

We cannot let pass without comment the important and paradoxical implication of the last of these points: anyone consistently possessing and demonstrating all of the first five would have little justification for regarding themselves as 'nothing special', yet it is this balance of humility with the pride and passion of a 'driven' leader that seems to us to be the distinguishing feature of inspirational headteachers in schools of all kinds and sizes. We will see evidence of similar characteristics in the primary headteachers featured in Chapters 5 and 6.

Conclusion

Personalizing learning for young people in schools, as explored in Chapter 2, is a hugely challenging endeavour. Its development requires a number of conducive factors to be in place in schools. One of the most important of these is undoubtedly committed and effective leadership. This chapter has introduced ideas related to distributed leadership and learning-centred leadership. These approaches are, we argue, the ones most likely to be conducive to personalizing learning. Like that concept, distributing leadership is not a straightforward idea or something that is easily implemented. We have sought to explore the complexity of effective leadership – reinforcing the notion that distributed leadership is not a singular phenomenon but a label for a range of approaches to leadership that stand in contrast to schools that emphasize leadership as solely vested in a headteacher operating in a hierarchical structure. Personalizing learning seeks to maximize the learning potential of individuals. Distributing leadership seeks to maximize the leadership potential of all staff so that the leadership capacity of a school is maximized, in order to create the most effective learning environment possible. The following chapter explores the relationship between personalized learning and distributed leadership, and the parallels between them.

Chapter 4

Parallels between personalizing learning and distributing leadership

Introduction

This chapter explores the links between personalizing learning and distributing leadership through overarching themes that are critical to both. First, we explore the concept of the learning journey – with the themes of direction and moral purpose, storying, shared values and participation. Second, we look at the qualities of relationships that are crucial to both leadership and learning. Third, we look at processes of learning – for leaders and learners – and fourth, we explore the personal qualities and competencies necessary for both. Our fifth and final section addresses the 'meta' theme(s) of power, autonomy and control that we bring to the foreground, since it permeates every aspect of leadership and learning.

Facilitating and leading learning: a journey metaphor

In Chapter 2 we looked at the key principles that Mosely and his colleagues (2005) identified as part of frameworks for thinking and learning that have been in use in the last 60 years. They include, as discussed: the domain of learning; the content of learning including objectives and products; the processes of learning, which were characterized by sequencing, hierarchy, types of thinking or learning, complexity and quality; and psychological aspects that include the notion of stages, structural features of cognition, dispositions, consciousness, orchestration or control, internalization and degree of learner autonomy. This substantial work supports the development of a 'journey metaphor', which is an important way of understanding both the different and similar elements of personalizing learning and of leadership.

In a learning journey, there is a person who, as a learner, has a sense of self, identity and story. This person has a motivation to learn something, and an objective or an outcome in mind. They move sequentially through a particular domain, relating to other learners, developing their own personal power to learn along the way. The nature of their relationships with others includes those who may mentor them, or instruct them, and those they may learn from and with. A learning journey is thus a complex process in a networked system, in which learning is distributed among the participants who are a 'community of travellers'. The same can be said of a 'leadership journey', which is, of course, also a learning journey. In this case, the outcome or goal is a preferred future that is, perhaps, encapsulated in a shared vision of what things will be like when a change or improvement has been implemented. Ideally, it will be a vision informed by shared and explicit values and a common understanding of the school's mission and purpose. It will be a vision that has to be co-constructed by those with vested interests. It will have been informed by a range of 'voices' and be an institutional narrative about which all feel a sense of ownership.

Learning and leadership can be conceptualized as parallel and inextricably linked journeys as illustrated in Figure 3, like intertwined DNA spirals. This model applies to adult learners as they learn to contribute to leadership and to young people as they develop the capacity to lead their own, and others', learning.

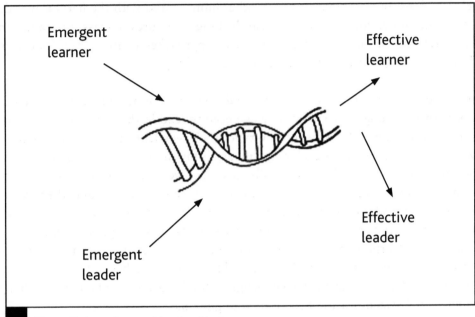

Figure 3: Learning and leadership journeys

Leadership, learning and moral purpose

As soon as we understand learning as a process in terms of 'direction' (which includes both time and change) then we encounter questions of moral purpose. Deep learning, like leadership, is about change and transformation, and although learning is often incremental – one small step at a time – overall and over time, learning leads to a changed state, or a changed way of being in the world. When learning is personal and personalized, then it can be transformational for the person concerned.

Tobin Hart (2001) identifies a map of deep knowing and learning, which begins with the accumulation of data and information, and moves through meaning making and creativity to the ability to act wisely, and at the deepest level, to personal and social transformation. Again, parallels with leadership are evident. What Hart describes as a 'movement towards wholeness' may be understood as the moral purpose of education. That is the well-being of the individual in a community – personal fulfilment, a life enriched through ongoing lifelong learning and the capacity and motivation to make a positive contribution to, and engagement with society – to become an informed and active citizen.

The field of leadership provides some rich ideas about such personal and social transformation. Senge et al. (2004) propose 'theory U' as a way of understanding the processes of profound personal and social change, necessary for leadership in 'the networked society', and for personal maturation and collective change. For him, change involves going into a deeper place, into a shift in awareness, which is at the heart of all creativity – it means a 'letting go' and a 'letting come', allowing new perceptions and 'ways of seeing' to emerge from an inner process of reflection and attention.

O'Sullivan (2003: 330) describes transformative learning in the following way: 'Transformative learning involves experiencing a deep, structural shift in the basic premise of thought, feelings and actions. Such a shift involves our understanding of ourselves and our self-locations; our relationships with other humans and with the natural world; our understanding of relations of power in interlocking structures of class, race and gender; our body awareness, our visions of alternative approaches to living; and our sense of possibilities for social justice and peace and personal joy.'

The processes of learning and leadership are deeply interconnected within this model of transformative learning. Learners of any age need to lead in their own learning through becoming aware of and taking responsibility for their own learning journey, acquiring the personal power to learn, and developing and attaining publicly valued competencies and learning outcomes. For teachers, leadership also involves commitment to their students, to the moral imperative of their professional lives (Fullan 2003) and their collective professional responsibility. For school leaders, a further layer is becoming aware of and taking responsibility for the school community's learning and improvement in a manner that leads to all learners in the system achieving their goals. Fullan's notion of 'moral imperative' also emphasizes leaders' responsibilities to learners beyond the specific school community in which they work. He challenges school leaders to contribute to change in the wider school system for the benefit of young people.

The idea that learning can lead to profound change in individuals and communities is an important one and leading and managing change is a core competence for survival and improvement. What is needed today is more than simply the accumulation of knowledge. Individuals routinely face complex demands and these require not only knowledge and skills, but also the strategies and routines needed to apply them as well as appropriate emotions and attitudes, and the effective management of all these components. The ability to deal with complex demands requires certain competencies – and these competencies necessarily include cognitive, behavioural, ethical and social components.

Haste (2001) identifies the overarching 'meta-competence' of being able to manage the tension between innovation and continuity. This is something that schools need to nurture and develop in their learners and, in our opinion, in those who contribute to the school's leadership capacity. She argues that in order to be able to manage this tension people need to use these additional competencies:

- adaptively assimilate changing technologies
- deal with ambiguity and diversity
- find and sustain community links

- manage motivation and emotion

- moral responsibility and citizenship.

This tension is creative for both leadership and learning. That is, by holding both ends of the polarity in tension – continuity and innovation – and not overbalancing towards either pole, something new is able to emerge. That may be new personal learning or it may be new organizational learning, and it emerges through leadership, a sense of a preferred future or learning outcome.

The 'stations' of the learning journey

Using the metaphor of 'learning as a journey', we suggest that there might be four 'stations' that require attention from learners and leaders, although not in any particular order and some stations will certainly need revisiting and could be attended to concurrently.

The first is the learning self, with its particular identity, nested sets of relationships, stories and aspirations. The second is the personal qualities, values, attitudes and dispositions for learning and leading – perhaps twenty-first century virtues. The third is publicly required and personally valued competencies – such as managing situations, being an active citizen or managing ambiguity. The fourth is the acquisition of publicly assessed and valued knowledge and know-how. Learning (including that in the context of leadership) and teaching require the mentored, selective attention to be given to these stations in a spiral sequence since they are interdependent and cumulative.

The *National Standards for Headteachers* (DfES 2004) provide one model for describing aspects of the second, third and fourth of these for school leaders and set out the competencies, attributes and knowledge required of school leaders in the following areas: shaping the future; leading, learning and teaching; developing self and working with others; managing the organization; securing accountability; and strengthening community. These are, for school leaders and aspiring leaders, assessed through the National Professional Qualification for Headteachers (NPQH 2004).

Leadership and learning are like the narration of a story in which the beginning and possible endings are held in mind as the story is being told. For example, the dynamic assessment of learning power allows the learner and their teacher to reflect backwards to the learning self, since it is deeply personal, and to project forwards as mediated scaffolding, towards the development of competencies and the acquisition of knowledge and know-how. The purpose of making judgements about, or assessments of, someone's learning power is to facilitate the movement between personal identity, choice and motivation and the processes and outcomes of learning. It is in this sense dynamic since it is both retrospective (diagnostic and reflective) and prospective (formative and motivational). It is about the narratable self – integrating identity and personhood with learning outcomes.

In terms of distributed leadership, account must be taken of the identities and stories of the learners, and the shared stories and values of the learning community, including young learners and adults. The qualities of leadership for learning require the same capacity to 'live within the learning story' as for learners themselves – leaders simply have a wider responsibility for other learners and for the direction of the whole learning community. The personal learning power of leaders and those contributing to leadership is as important as that which they seek to nurture in others – and the outcomes of the learning community need to be congruent with and integral to its organizational identity and values. It is through developing their own learning power that leaders develop their personal leadership capacity and, therefore, increase the overall leadership capacity of the school in which they work. Concepts, or learning power dimensions introduced in Chapter 2 (strategic awareness, creativity, meaning making, critical curiosity, changing and learning, learning relationships and resilience), have equal significance when applied to leadership and, indeed, when considered in the context of a learning institution.

In particular, leaders cannot lead without strategic awareness. Effective leadership requires creative, lateral and innovative approaches. For leaders, curiosity and meaning making relate to the identification of issues and concerns that need addressing and the development of a coherent and valid interpretation of those issues and concerns – that is, the story constructed about the school's journey of improvement.

Creativity is undoubtedly needed by leaders in dealing with the complexity of twenty-first century schools. As the National Advisory Committee on Creative and Cultural Education (NACCCE) said in their significant report to ministers, *All Our Futures* (1999: 102), 'Such (outstanding) headteachers are creative, risk takers. They value and use creativity in their own thinking, in management, in teaching and learning and in the curriculum. They hold fast to the conviction that creativity in all its forms must significantly affect the children and teachers in their schools and in their futures.'

Resilience, it could be argued, is certainly as important for leaders as learners, especially as they seek to implement new initiatives and improvements such as personalizing learning – leaders must remain optimistic, committed and motivated when others may be feeling less enthusiastic about change. They must persevere when the going gets tough – but they must do this through coaching and role modelling rather than coercion. They should not, of course, accept change blindly but be open to feedback from others and adapt accordingly.

In all of these dimensions, the leader plays a part in role modelling that will influence all learners in the institution. They should be seen as lead learners who know themselves as learners and leaders. This learning-centred approach contributes to a conducive ethos and climate for all learners.

The centrality of relationships

Both leadership and learning are about active participation, by individuals and teams in the processes of the journey. The quality of the relationships between learners, teachers, leaders and the wider communities of which they are a part is a critical success factor, but it is hard to quantify or measure as an outcome. This is partly because relationships are experienced, and experience, by definition, is unique to each individual.

The quality of relationships within a learning community form part of its 'social capital'. Putnam (2000) defines social capital as 'the collective value of all "social networks" and the inclinations that arise from these networks to do things for each other', and he argues that social capital is a key component to building and maintaining democracy. Fukuyama (1995) says that social capital is the existence of a certain set of informal values or norms shared among members of a group that permit cooperation among them. Paying attention to the quality of relationships in a learning community is essential for both effective learning and for distributed leadership, because relationships are a 'form of capital' that affects both the processes and the outcomes of learning.

The network of relationships that learners operate within includes their peers and friends, older and younger learners; their teachers and other staff; their immediate families and the wider communities and traditions of which they may be a part. Teachers and school leaders conduct relationships with their students, their peers, their parents and carers and the local community – with people they are responsible to and for. They also relate through networks to the wider educational community, including politicians.

In other words, all of the participants live within a networked relational system, which coheres through a variety of relationships, bounded by shared purposes and/or interests. Schluter (2003) identifies relational 'proximity' as a key indicator of the ways in which people get to know and understand each other. Proximity can be expressed through directness – the degree of face to face interaction; continuity over time; multiplexity – contact in more than one role; parity – the degree of 'equality' and commonality – the extent of shared purpose and values. We would add common interests as well.

A key quality of relationships is trust, which we discussed in Chapter 3. Trust is a relationship of such quality that both parties are confident that it can withstand the challenges of inequality, risk, uncertainty and difference (Bond 2004). In order to learn something, the learner has to move beyond their comfort zone and often has to face uncertainty and risk. Furthermore the teacher often does know, where the learner does not, and this is an unequal balance. In order to move on and to follow a vision, there are also elements of uncertainty and risk both for leaders and those who follow and for teams committing to a shared but uncertain new future that they have collectively agreed to construct. The characteristic of trust, or the confidence that these things can be faced and negotiated, and that the relationship will not break down through abuse or fragility, appears to be a critical thread in the ecology of a learner-centred environment for learners and leaders. It could even be argued that where there is no risk, uncertainty or inequality, there is unlikely to be learning and not much need for leadership.

For learning and leadership, relationships need to allow for both affirmation and challenge. People who feel safe, and know that they belong and are valued, are more likely to take risks and allow themselves to be challenged than those who feel threatened or excluded in some way. An emotionally literate school is one in which both learners and teachers feel 'it's OK for me to be here' (Hadden et al. 2005) and this is as important for leadership as it is for learning. Distributed leadership and personalized learning both require a culture that is deeply affirming of the learning identities of all members in the system – a 'one size fits all' culture will not work.

However, being learning centred requires an appropriate degree of challenge. Both of us have been involved in research that indicates the centrality of trust. In research into the ecology of learning power (Deakin Crick 2007a), the relationships between learners and teachers were also characterized by the challenge to move forwards – the amount of challenge possible was directly related to the quality of trust in the relationship. Students needed to trust that their teachers could teach them, and in order to lead, leaders need to earn the trust of those they lead, so that both can be appropriately challenged to change and grow. Research into distributed leadership (Ritchie 2004; 2007a), as outlined in Chapter 3, also highlighted the importance of trust among teachers to successful distributed leadership.

Another element that is crucial to relationships in learning and to leadership, is time and space. It takes time and the right sort of space to listen to the other person, and to do the sort of inner reflection that is necessary for learning and changing, and for leadership – for example, co-construction of a preferred future or analysis of professional development needs in the context of coaching. Very often in schools, time is carved up in a way that is not friendly to learning or to leadership. Palmer (1998: 73–77) writes about the sorts of space necessary for learning:

- The space should be bounded and open. Without limits it is difficult to see how learning can occur. Explorations need a focus. However, spaces need to be open as well – open to the many paths down which discovery may take us. 'If boundaries remind us that our journey has a destination, openness reminds us that there are many ways to reach that end.' More than that, openness allows us to find other destinations.

- The space should be hospitable and 'charged'. We may find the experience of space strange and fear that we may get lost. Learning spaces need to be hospitable – 'inviting as well as open, safe and trustworthy as well as free'. When exploring we need places to rest and find nourishment. But if we feel too safe, then we may stay on the surface of things. Space needs to be charged so that we may know the risks involved in looking at the deeper things of life.

- The space should invite the voice of the individual and the voice of the group. Learning spaces should invite people to speak truly and honestly. People need to be able to express their thoughts and feelings. This involves building environments where individuals can speak and groups can gather and give voice to their concerns and passions.

- The space should honour the 'little' stories of those involved and the 'big' stories of the disciplines and tradition. Learning spaces should honour people's experiences, give room to stories about everyday life. At the same time, we need to connect these stories with the larger picture. We need to be able to explore how our personal experiences fit in with those of others; and how they may relate to more general 'stories' and understandings about life.

- The space should support solitude and surround it with the resources of community. Learning demands both solitude and community. People need time alone to reflect and absorb. Their experiences and struggles need to be respected. At the same time, they need to be able to call upon and be with others. We need conversations in which our ideas are tested and biases challenged.

- The space should welcome both silence and speech. Silence gives us the chance to reflect on things. It can be a sort of speech 'emerging from the deepest part of ourselves, of others, of the world'. At the same time we need to be able to put things into words so that we gain a greater understanding and to make concrete what we may share in silence.

This sets a challenging agenda when viewed in the context of both learning and leadership and, for example, the leadership and management of teams. It suggests the need to deal creatively with tensions between freedom and limits. In thinking about personalizing learning it raises the question of the degree of flexibility and how this can be managed for each learner and the learning situation. It challenges us to consider, at the institutional level, who is the custodian of the knowledge learned/taught.

It also raises issues related to culture, ethos and climate (Bell and Ritchie 1999). The reality of schools and the pressures within which some operate make it very difficult to address some, let alone all, of the above in classrooms and staffrooms. However, effective learning, especially learning that is personalized, requires such spaces and a conducive ethos, climate and culture. This has implications for organizational structures that also need attention, which we will explore further in the next chapter.

The nature of learning relationships

The quality of interaction between learner and teacher or mentor is important in the process of learning itself. Vygotsky (1978) talks about the zone of proximal development (ZPD), which he describes as 'the distance between the actual developmental level as determined by independent problem solving and the level of potential development as determined through problem solving under adult guidance, or in collaboration with more capable peers'. This implies that learning is framed by social interaction and collaborative problem solving. Sociocultural theorists increasingly conceptualize learning as distributed, interactive, contextual and the result of the learner's participation in a community of practice (Chang-Wells and Wells 1993; Cole and Engerstrom 1993; John-Steiner et al. 1994; Rogoff 1994). What, we wonder, is the equivalent to a ZPD when thinking about adult learning and the role of leaders supporting others?

The processes of learning are scaffolded in the interactions of the learning encounter that involves the learner and the teacher (or mentor) attending to the person, the process and the outcome of learning and selectively moving between them. Indeed, the term 'teacher' may be more accurately replaced with the term 'learning guide', or 'leading learner' since the purpose of learning is for the learner to begin to take responsibility for their own learning journey. This requires a pedagogical relationship that can:

- recognize the person of the learner, his or her intentionality, authority, relationships and story

- allow these to initiate, shape and motivate the learning process

- include reflection on process as an essential component of what is learned (learning about learning)

57

- free the learner to span and connect pre-existing forms and stores of knowledge

- enable the learning to relate – and achieve a purpose of value – to the (accountable) world.

When leaders support colleagues in taking risks as they implement change they are often scaffolding their learning outside of what we might regard as a comfort zone. We see this in coaching and mentoring relationships. As teachers are coached by more experienced colleagues in personalizing the learning of learners for whom they are responsible there are parallel learning relationships operating in which one person is facilitating the learning of another but both, potentially, can learn from the process.

Increasingly in schools we are seeing a blurring and extending of boundaries of relationships. Teachers become learners and learners become facilitators of others' learning. Leaders become team members and others (teachers or non-teachers), capable of taking on leadership responsibilities, take the lead. In Chapter 3, 'extending boundaries' was explored as a key concept in relation to distributed leadership. The same can be argued in the context of personalizing learning when we explore learning, teaching and assessment. In schools, leadership essentially creates the conditions in which professionals can exercise judgements and form learning relationships with each other and with young people.

Assessment as relational

The practice that most determines what actually goes on in learning and teaching and in the school curriculum as a whole is assessment (Broadfoot 1998). Within a learning-centred culture, assessment is an act of leadership to the extent that it points the way forwards for the learner, and is invitational and affirming of the person who is learning. The dynamic assessment of learning power is important in making these connections since it reflects backwards to the learning self, which is deeply personal and forwards as mediated scaffolding, towards the development of competencies and the acquisition of knowledge and know-how. The purpose of making judgements about, or assessments of, someone's learning power is to facilitate the movement between personal identity, choice and motivation and the processes and outcomes of learning. It is in this sense dynamic since it is both retrospective (diagnostic and reflective) and prospective (formative and motivational).

Within a learning-centred system there is a spectrum, of what can be assessed, which ranges from internal, deeply personal and subjective knowledge at one end (the beginning) to external, objective, publicly agreed and therefore formal knowledge, at the other end (the conclusion).

At the deeply personal end of the spectrum an external assessor cannot judge 'right or wrong' but can simply listen, affirm, reflect back and question, making an equally personal – even intuitive – judgement about such things as authenticity, engagement, commitment. This judgement can be validated only by the learner. At the external or public end, an external assessor can judge 'right or wrong' in many domains, both in terms of the specialized knowledge content of relevant, pre-existing curricula and the degree to which the communicative purpose of the learning has been achieved by the language, form and presentation of its outcome. While the learner can self-assess the work against these external criteria (and will have done if well coached in the practice of assessment for learning), these judgements can be validated only by an external assessor representing the community of expertise in that particular subject. The pedagogical and relational skill is in nurturing and leading the learner in his or her journey from one end of the spectrum to the other, giving safe passage to the tender and uncertain sense of personal authority in the attitudes, dispositions, beliefs and personal motivations with which he or she embarked.

Is there an equivalent process to assessment for learning in leadership development? We think there may be, in particular in coaching relationships (discussed in Chapter 3). A coach will support a colleague (the coachee) in identifying strengths and areas for development. That support should also lead to the setting of appropriate targets that can be reviewed at a later date. It is an example where peer and self-assessment for formative purposes are to the fore, although it does run the risk of confusing assessment and evaluation. There may also be a case for seeing performance management as another process with parallels to assessment – in this example, at the more formal and, perhaps, external end of the spectrum discussed above and therefore potentially more problematic.

The person who learns and leads

Palmer (1998: 4) argues that we often ask the question of what we should teach, or whom we should teach and sometimes even why we should teach, but says: 'Seldom, if ever, do we ask the "who" question – who is the self that teaches? How does the quality of my selfhood form – or deform – the way I relate to my students, my subject, my colleagues, my world? How can educational institutions sustain and deepen the selfhood from which good teaching comes?'

The 'personhood of the teacher' is one of the most important, and yet underrated, elements of educational reform. We all remember particular teachers – what they looked like, how they made us feel, how it felt to be with them – but we can rarely remember the content of what they taught us. Palmer (1998; 2000; 2004) draws our attention eloquently to the need to attend to our inner selves as educators, since good teaching is so much more than technique. It 'comes from the identity and integrity of the teacher'. This means that teachers need to both know themselves, and to be seeking to live life as well as they can. Good teachers are, thus, connected, able to be in touch with themselves, with their students and their subjects – and they act in ways that further their own and other people's well-being.

Palmer (1998: 2) says: 'Teaching, like any truly human activity, emerges from one's inwardness, for better or worse. As I teach, I project the condition of my soul onto my students, my subject, and our way of being together...When I do not know myself, I cannot know who my students are. I will see them through a glass darkly, in the shadows of my unexamined life – and when I cannot see them clearly, I cannot teach them well. When I do not know myself, I cannot know my subject – not at the deepest levels of embodied, personal meaning. I will know it only abstractly, from a distance, a congeries of concepts as far removed from the world as I am from personal truth.'

All professionals hold values that underpin and inform their practice as teachers and leaders. These values are not always made explicit, but knowing yourself means understanding those personal values and the extent to which they are lived out in professional practice. Whitehead (1989) and others have since recognized the extent to which professionals' values are often denied in practice as a result of the daily dilemmas they face, the complex contexts in which they work and the values implicit in national policies, for example, assessment regimes and practices and in some school interpretations of those requirements. They can become, in his words, 'living contradictions'.

Learning and leading require self-awareness, emotional intelligence, creativity and practical intelligence. In Chapter 2 we looked at some of these qualities as necessary for personalizing learning. Emotional literacy is sensitivity and skill in both intra-personal awareness and interpersonal relationships and this is particularly important in leadership. Salovey and Mayer (1990) developed a model of emotional intelligence with five main domains:

- self-awareness (the basis for all the rest)
- emotional management
- self-motivation
- empathy
- social competence.

Effective interpersonal communication is a seamless integration of a wide range of behaviours that support the ability to build positive relationships. Such integration demonstrates flexibility, range and balance as well as skill, and has been described as 'functional fluency' (Temple 2002; 2004). An analysis of interpersonal communication can reveal habits or tendencies that hinder both learning and leadership. For example, Temple (ibid.) describes how some people do not realize that care can be harmful. One secondary school year head was wearing herself out by doing too much for her pupils, rather than helping them to help themselves. Teachers frequently assume that being strict means being negative and authoritarian and it is a relief to them to realize that they can achieve control through creating structure, which is empowering, firm and inspiring. They also find it useful to differentiate between compliance and cooperation – helping children to be resilient and assertive, rather than submissive and passive.

As Temple (2004: 11) says: 'The main tool of any teacher in building classroom relationships is his or her own self. This means that personal development for teachers is synonymous with professional development. Self awareness is the key factor.'

For learning and leading, this understanding and these capacities are crucial since learning is about the other person taking ownership of and responsibility for their own learning journey, rather than fitting them into a particular mould. Personalization and distributed leadership support personal and community empowerment.

Power, autonomy and control

The themes of power, responsibility, autonomy and control or freedom have been implicit in much of the discussion so far. At one level, debates about these issues in society have been taking place for thousands of years and will do so for as long as society exists. At a more simple level, however, one of the assumptions of our discussions has been the values of participation and inclusion – which in turn attribute value to each human being, regardless of race, gender, religion, economic status and so on. They also assume basic rights of human beings for learning, growth and self-direction.

Such values require social conditions and structures that enable the flourishing of human beings in all their relationships, including with themselves as learners over time. Leadership that serves to 'close down' the humanity of another, or a group of others, is abusive. The inner life of learners, the challenge of becoming responsible learners and leaders, are key elements of human community that require power to be operated, by those who have more of it, in ways that are autonomy supportive, rather than controlling.

Personalized learning and distributed leadership require schools to be characterized by what Habermas (1972) calls hermeneutical and emancipatory, rather than only by instrumental, interests. This idea derives from his understanding of the connection between human interests and knowledge. He identifies three interests – instrumental, hermeneutic and emancipatory – each of which he identifies with a type of human knowing.

The first interest he associates with the knowledge generated by natural and analytic sciences such as physics and mathematics. This is the technical interest of prediction and control of objectified processes, or instrumental action, which may show up in the learning community in terms of organization, timetabling and many aspects of a high stakes assessment system. Habermas associates the second interest with the knowledge developed by the human disciplines such as history or the social sciences. This is the practical interest of intersubjective understanding of the conduct of life in the context of the human social world. This interest might show up in the learning community in terms of communication and interpretation of each other, or in the social and human sciences. Finally, Habermas associates the third interest with the knowledge generated by what he calls the critical sciences. This is the emancipatory interest of becoming free from the seemingly natural (but actually constructed) constraints of ideologies, world views and value systems. Individually, this interest might show itself in terms of the construction of a learning identity and a learning pathway that is unique and not dominated by social expectations, interpretations, and roles. In the learning community it might show up in terms of locally determined solutions and directions.

We think that Habermas's distinction between different knowledge interests is important for understanding the sort of knowledge bases and power relations we believe to be crucial for personalized learning and distributed leadership. In our view, strategic rationality and hermeneutic rationality should be operated in the service of human emancipation and well-being. Such a system will encourage the development of self-aware learners and professionally competent teachers, since the full range of their humanity will be available, encouraged and accessible in their learning, at both a personal and shared or communal level.

Conclusion

This chapter has provided an analysis of the similarities and differences that are involved in processes related to personalizing learning and distributing leading. Both areas are complex and not singular phenomena. Leadership and intelligence are, for example, both fluid notions that remain somewhat contested. The discussion has explored this complexity through metaphorical consideration of the learning journeys involved in both: the significance of relationships; the processes in which individuals engage; the personal qualities and competencies involved; and the implications of power, autonomy and control.

Through this discussion we have highlighted the outcomes that result for learners related to enhanced and extended skills, knowledge and understanding and strategies for, and commitment to, their own and others' future learning. For teachers outcomes include increased capacity to lead and manage change for the benefit of others. The outcomes for schools as learning organizations are more flexibility to respond to diverse community and learners' needs.

Outcomes for school systems from simultaneous moves to personalizing learning and distributing leadership are, we suggest, increased capacity for change and improvements, especially from those not normally associated with system-wide change – an enhanced and informed professional voice that fosters professional competence and engagement in policy issues. More sophisticated and metacognitive engagement with these significant drivers for school improvement can positively impact on schools through increasing the leadership and learning capacity of institutions and the individuals they comprise.

In the following chapters we will address the particular implications for the roles of headteachers (Chapter 5), subject leaders and middle leaders (Chapter 6) and teachers (Chapter 7).

Chapter 5

'Letting go': the role of headteachers

Introduction

This chapter focuses on the role of the headteacher as the 'designated' (Jackson 2002a) or 'symbolic' (Murphy et al. 1993) leader who has a key role in facilitating distributed leadership. In Chapter 3 we recognized the complexity of leadership. According to Jackson (2002a: 2), 'It is as much akin to potential energy as it is to kinetic. Leadership is about the latent as well as the currently lived and enacted expressions of leading. As metaphor, it has much in common with the notion of intellectual capital – the potentially banked and available capacity to be drawn, and the interest that can be added! As such it potentially exists very widely within an organization.'

In this chapter, we explore how that potential can be released. As we argued earlier, moves to personalizing learning require a paradigm shift. It is therefore unsurprising that we also question whether existing school organization/management structures are conducive to distributed leadership and personalizing learning. We are of a view that they are not and that they need to be reconceptualized and adapted in many schools to make them fit for the purpose of expanding leadership capacity for personalized learning.

Distributed leadership is not something that operates in one direction – it can be top down, bottom-up or have a lateral manifestation. Enquiry teams, where leadership of the group is collective or rotated, are examples of the latter. Distributed leadership can be inhibited by top-down structures with regard to aspects of hierarchy and power that they can foster. Structures conducive to distributed leadership are likely to be fluid and flexible and adaptive to the changing context in which they are created and used.

Effective distributed leadership, as we noted in Chapter 3, is invitational rather than imposed. Those without designated titles and, indeed, those with them, need to want to lead and their 'right to lead' has also to be granted by followers if it is to be effective. We explore the creative tensions that headteachers face and consider the relationship between personal power and institutional power. We will argue that the former needs to exceed the latter for them to maximize the impact of their leadership.

Headteachers' roles with regard to distributed leadership

A headteacher's task according to Jackson (2002a: 2) is to 'harness, focus, liberate, empower leadership towards common purposes'. They do this through 'creating the spaces, the contexts and the opportunities for expansion, enhancement and growth amongst all'. Senge (1990) suggested that in 'learning organizations' leaders should leave their status at the door. Jackson (2002a) reminds us that in hierarchical structures it is necessary for others to leave the designated leader's status at the door too.

Headteachers may seek to distribute leadership for a number of reasons and in a number of ways. These may be strategic, pragmatic, opportunistic, incremental or cultural (MacBeath et al. 2004). We consider the latter to be essential for sustained change to result from distributing leadership.

In Chapter 3, based on one of our research studies, we identified characteristics of heads in schools where distributed leadership was judged to be embedded. These have resonance with some of Murphy et al. (1993) – metaphors of leaders as social and organizational architects. Headteachers have to design (with others) and implement the organizational structures that will support the engagement of others in leadership as well as structures that are conducive to personalized learning – a complex task, which is likely to remain 'work in progress' given the constantly changing context in which schools operate.

We noted that leaders should 'live out their values' in their professional lives – as both leader and (where appropriate) as follower or team member. This is where the personal power of the head needs to be at the fore. This role modelling as a means of building the capacity of others also requires them to live out their professional lives as 'lead learners'. They need to make their commitment to and understanding of their own learning explicit. Below, we discuss further the notion of 'headteacher as learner' and consider the idea of treating learning and leadership as inextricably related.

Release of leadership potential in others clearly has an interpersonal dimension – it needs facilitating, nurturing and support, again focusing on the personal as opposed to the institutional dimensions of the role. We regard coaching as an effective process for doing this and return to it later in this chapter. It requires and in turn supports the creation of trusting relationships and the co-construction of shared values and sense of purpose. Dialogue is essential for providing opportunities for exploring values and the moral imperative of the school's endeavours. It also allows the leader to hold others accountable to the explicit and shared values of the school with regard, for example, to personalized learning.

Allowing others to take fuller responsibility for significant school developments can feel threatening to the designated leader, who is ultimately responsible for the school. Creating structures conducive to distributed leadership and giving up the power that comes with traditional hierarchical models of leadership involves taking risks and requires a degree of moral courage. As already noted, though, the head's success in 'letting go' (Senge et al. 2004) is dependent on others allowing this to happen. This is not helped by traditional views of headteachers that involve what might be seen as the 'singular identity' model of school leader and the implications this has for others' dependency on the one leader. For these and other reasons, letting go is potentially the hardest part of distributing leadership for some heads.

Headteachers' learning journeys

We have already made it clear that, for us, learning and leadership are related in complex but essential ways – they are interdependent. A good leader needs to be a good learner and a good learner is likely to have more potential to be an effective leader than someone less open to learning.

In Chapter 4, we introduced the metaphor of learning journeys. Headteachers' learning journeys have often been long and involved working in various roles and in varying contexts.

The NCSL recognizes various stages in headteachers' learning journeys including:

- Emergent leadership – when a teacher is beginning to take on management and leadership responsibilities and is building personal leadership capacity.

- Established leadership – comprising assistant and deputy heads who are experienced leaders. During this phase, institutional dimensions become more significant although building personal capacity remains vital.

- Entry to headship – including a teacher's preparation for and induction into the senior post in a school. This is possibly the most challenging stage and when gaps in personal capacity can be exposed and the institutional context and constraints can dominate.

- Advanced leadership – the stage at which school leaders look to widen their experience, to refresh themselves and to update their skills. It is heads in this stage who, because of changes in schooling in the last few years, are the ones having to re-evaluate their understanding of leadership and adopt new approaches.

- Consultant leadership – when an able and experienced leader is ready to put something back into the profession by taking on training, mentoring or inspection. This stage receives the least attention in the context of this book.

We suggest that a hallmark of strong and effective leaders is their readiness to recognize that the more they know the more they need to know. Different stages provide differing opportunities to learn and require different outcomes, because the purposes will be different. An advanced or consultant leader, as well as perhaps already knowing much more about the structures, processes, routines and procedures of management than an emergent leader, might also have acquired the mental space to develop a real fascination for the personal elements of learning and leadership that reside in the uniqueness of individuals and their responses to change, the unpredictability of moments and the insights they offer. Headteachers' learning is often ad hoc and, for some, rarely made explicit. The learning may be through experience – reflection 'in' or 'on' action (Schon 1983) – and through dialogue. Learning through doing the job and through the ongoing conversations that are part of every head's daily life, with fellow professionals, young people, their parents and carers and others, provide professional lifelong active learning. In particular, it is through these learning conversations that some of the most important personal qualities of heads come to the fore – for example, active and open-ended listening. In other words, a leader can 'distribute' the power of personalized learning by involving and engaging others in the demonstration of a very personal kind of critical curiosity.

If headteachers are to provide role models for others as lead learners they need to acknowledge and maximize the range of learning opportunities that they have. Such opportunities can be informal or formal, explicit or implicit, individual or social, shallow or deep, facilitated or self-led, short term or long term. Formal settings, with scope for 'reflection on action', include:

- teaching and interactions with pupils
- monitoring/observation of colleagues
- coaching/mentoring of colleagues
- in-school collaboration with staff in planning /team contexts
- staff development – school- or centred-based (e.g. local authority or university locations).
- formal professional development, for example, NCSL programmes/Higher Education Institution (HEI) provision
- networks and partnerships
- international visits
- school self-evaluation and dialogue with school improvement partners
- school-based enquiries.

Informal opportunities, such as those presented by (apparently) unplanned conversations and off duty social discourse can be more powerful, by being sensed as natural and received as authentic, without any palpable design upon the listener.

It is through all these interactions, particularly those that involve dialogue with other professionals within and beyond the school, that the headteachers' sense of direction and understanding of the moral purpose of their professional lives emerge and are refined. Nothing is more likely to inspire and engage colleagues in their own leadership development than discovering they can play an active and significant part in the learning journey of their headteacher.

One of us has been working with networks of headteachers for some years with the explicit aim of fostering their deep learning to improve their leadership and, consequently, to impact on the quality of learning and teaching in their schools. Several of these groups have addressed improvements related to what is now embraced within personalizing learning such as curriculum development, assessment for learning, innovative use of ICT. These have included long-standing networks of heads (a small schools group that has been meeting for six years); funded projects with diverse networks of heads focusing on school-based enquiries (for example, Ritchie and Ikin 2000) and smaller learning sets with specific foci (Ritchie 2006). The contribution of these developments to school self-evaluation and the perceived benefits to participants have been discussed elsewhere (Ritchie 2007b).

Some of the most difficult moments on a learning journey involve managing apparently irreconcilable tensions. An obvious example, faced by most headteachers at some time, is the tension between the interests of the school community and those of an individual member whose behaviour and attitudes seriously threaten to undermine it. Palmer (2004) describes a learning opportunity designed to help with such moments. It is based on the 400-year-old Quaker practice called a 'Clearness Committee', in which colleagues 'think together', asking only 'open, honest questions', forming 'personal connections' and using 'blame free, truth telling zones' to help each other to become 'more productive in general and more resilient in a crisis'. There are some parallels here to learning sets.

Headteachers' learning selves

Headteachers' learning, like that of young people, is influenced by many factors, including how well they know themselves and the 'identity' they construct for themselves as learners. All learners have 'life narratives' that impact on their learning and leadership capacity and biographical factors can have both constructive and inhibiting influences. An effective leader and learner is aware of these and seeks to minimize the inhibiting and maximize the positive drivers that are a consequence of previous experiences.

Some leaders are confident enough of their identity as learners to share it with others. Some examples from the networks discussed above, include heads who share specific aspects of themselves as learners, such as the head who learned to play the bagpipes and shared, regularly in assemblies, the progress he made and barriers he encountered in his learning. While playing the bagpipes has no direct benefit to the head's leadership, in a learning-centred school it allowed him to role model himself as a learner and how seriously he was taking his learning. It also illustrated how difficult learning can sometimes be and modelled resilience, a critical aspect of effective learning. Another kept a public learning journal in the staffroom and sought to record daily what he had learned from his professional activity. Others shared progress on their masters or doctorate research. These are ways in which heads provide excellent role models as lead learners. In one school, featured in Ritchie (2006), the head, Wendy Davey, goes as far as putting 'Head Learner' on her door and makes her role as lead learner in the school explicit symbolically and through her behaviour and engagement with other learners, both young and old.

There are lessons here for those who work with heads to support their development. Dialogues between heads and with others who facilitate their learning can, and perhaps should, focus on how the 'learning heads' see themselves.

Headteachers' learning usually involves a social context and their learning is enhanced or inhibited by relationships. Ideally, these will be genuine, pedagogic relationships that foster deep learning – for example, in a mentoring relationship, where a more experienced head mentors one new to the role, or a Higher Education (HE) tutor supports a headteacher in the context of research for an MA. However, genuine pedagogic relationships and learning conversations do not just happen – they need to be encouraged and require commitment and effort. They require, in fact, the same qualities that we identified in Chapter 2 as characterizing all effective learning relationships: trust, affirmation and challenge. Without trust, it is hard to take the risk of rising to challenge. Without affirmation, it is hard to sustain the effort of responding to challenge. Without challenge, there is little opportunity to gain affirmation or deepen trust. One of the benefits of facilitated networks, that their participants have regularly cited, is that the anticipation of regular testing of their learning against the critical friendships of detached fellow professionals keeps them focused and engaged. Collaborative learning within schools can be seen as a prerequisite of distributed leadership and expanding leadership capacity. The headteacher who is intent upon expanding leadership capacity will, at times, be facilitating that sort of collaborative learning and, at other times, modelling learning as 'just another' member of the team, or as a follower. In this way, the cultivation of professional learning relationships can develop into the culture of a learning community.

The concept of 'critical friendship' becomes important here in thinking about the way in which professionals facilitate each other's learning. It signifies a relationship that is characterized by trust, affirmation and challenge, in which a tacit dissatisfaction with the status quo takes nothing away from colleagues' mutual regard and implies that a shared, restless sense of the purpose of improvement has become at least as important as recognizing and celebrating achievement.

Headteachers, like many educational professionals, tend towards 'action learning', sometimes based on school-based enquiry methods. Most of the networking initiatives mentioned above engaged the heads in such enquiries, drawing on action research approaches (Ritchie 2006). Essentially the process is a cyclical one in which heads identify a concern (perhaps where their values are 'denied in action'); plan systematically to improve the situation; implement the changes and collect evidence of its impact; evaluate that impact and consider next steps. It involves reflection *on*, not merely *in* action and is what Schon (1983) describes as 'double loop learning'.

The approaches described provide a model of 'demand-led' learning since the foci for enquiries are under the control of the learner – the learning is facilitated but essentially gives the individual autonomy. This is certainly personalized learning for leaders.

These learning journeys can be related as 'stories' in order for the learning to be shared with others and, perhaps, enhanced through communication and co-creation of the narrative. Revisiting learning to share it through 'storying' with others can lead to deeper learning through reflection and reflexivity. One group of heads with which one of us worked disseminated their learning through a publication entitled *Telling Tales of School Improvement* (Ritchie and Ikin 2000). The title reinforces the way in that their journeys were being shared through stories aimed at being significant for others. They became the way in which headteachers could share, with others, answers to the questions of how and why they lead in the way they do and how that changed over time. Through their stories and the enquiries and discussion within the network that led to them, they were talking through their values and aspirations – sharing and understanding their learning and leading selves.

Headteachers' personal qualities, values, attitudes and dispositions

The nature of personal qualities that are needed for headship is the subject of considerable literature. It is worth mentioning again how attracted we are to the list (quoted in Chapter 3 on p48) proposed by Woods (2002) in his research on what he described as 'enchanted headteachers'.

A more analytical list of qualities comes from the Hay McBer organization (see Figure 4). This has been influential in informing the NCSL leadership programmes and implies a broader view but one, perhaps, that is less focused on the personal and human-centred qualities of school leaders.

Analytical thinking	The ability to think logically, break things down and recognise cause and effect.
Challenge and support	A commitment to do everything possible for each pupil and to enable all pupils to be successful.
Confidence	A real belief in one's ability to be effective and to take on challenges.
Developing potential	The drive to develop others' capabilities and help them realise their full potential.
Drive for improvement	Relentless energy for setting and meeting challenging targets, for pupils and the school.
Holding people accountable	The drive and ability to set clear expectations and parameters and to hold others accountable for performance.
Impact and influence	The ability and the drive to produce positive outcomes by impressing and influencing others.
Information seeking	A drive to find out more and get to the heart of things; intellectual curiosity.
Initiative	The drive to act now to anticipate and pre-empt events.
Integrity	Being consistent and fair. Keeping one's word.
Personal conviction	A passionate commitment to education, based on deeply held values and beliefs, or born out of a desire to serve pupils, parents and the community.
Respect for others	An underlying belief that individuals matter, and deserve respect.

Strategic thinking	The ability to see patterns and make links, even when there is lot of detail, and to see the big picture.
Teamworking	The ability to work with others to achieve shared goals.
Transformational leadership	The drive and the ability to take the role of leader, provide clear direction, and enthuse and motivate others.
Understanding the environment	The ability to understand and make positive use of the relationships or social and cultural differences within the school or in organisations in the wider community.
Understanding others	The drive and an ability to understand others, and why they behave as they do.

Figure 4: Leadership characteristics (Hobby 2001)

The danger of such prescriptions is that aspiring leaders might reasonably feel that they could never match up to them. That is another reason for emphasizing the dynamic nature of the learning story in leadership development. Just as Barnes (1975) says in relation to teaching, it is not much use asking people 'to arrive without having travelled'.

In order to underline the relationship between leadership and learning that is so fundamental to our purpose in this book, we propose another framework for exploring headteachers' (and other leaders') dispositions to learning and leadership that we referred to in Chapter 2 (Deakin Crick 2006). Figure 5 describes the seven dimensions of Learning Power as they were adapted by a group of heads involved in the Bristol Leaders of Learning (BriLL) Project (Ritchie 2006). They were used to support and strengthen leaders in developing their own values, dispositions and attitudes for learning in the context of leading change:

Changing and Learning – Leaders/learners who are strong in this dimension know that learning is itself learned and they can become more effective leaders through this. They recognise themselves as dynamic learners and leaders who change over time in response to changing circumstances and challenges. They celebrate their learning and the impact it has on them as leaders. Leaders have a willingness to recognise and seek to address gaps in their knowledge. They are able to be resourceful in order to find solutions. They use as much current information as possible to inform decisions and recognise the value of continual reflection.

Curiosity – Effective leaders/learners are inquisitive, reflective and prepared to consider a range of ideas, different points of view and possibilities. Curiosity in learning reflects an openness and willingness to consider the ideas of others, a degree of humility and an acceptance that there are many things we do not fully understand. Curiosity in learning is based on a recognition that we learn best through enquiry based activities based on what interests them and on solving problems. Leaders have a desire to delve deeper to further their understanding.

Meaning Making – Effective learners/leaders are on the look out for links between what they are learning and what they know from experience and previous learning. They are good at 'making sense' of whatever happens. They connect learning about what it means to be an effective leader with other experiences in a range of contexts, with a strong sense of how the steps they are taking further the 'story' of where they and their school have come from and where they have got to so far on that journey.

Creativity – Creative leaders as learners are 'playful' with ideas. They like to explore new boundaries and will often encourage others to reflect on ideas and their experience. They are willing to take risks in their learning, where the outcomes may not be defined. They are particularly good at generating ideas, though they may need others to assist in accomplishing the task. They recognise the need to take the time to look at a problem from many perspectives, often inviting people to offer opinions or experience. They will use their imagination in finding the most suitable solutions. They follow their intuition in their learning and will sometimes act more on instinct than on hard evidence.

Resilience – Resilient leaders/learners enjoy challenges and are willing to give it a go even if the outcome and the way to proceed are initially uncertain. When the going gets tough, lead learners get learning. They persist when things are getting difficult and persevere in finding ways forward, accepting an alternative route may be necessary. Lead learners recognise that all learners, including themselves find learning difficult at times being experienced in and able to manage the feelings involved.

Strategic Awareness – Effective leaders as strategic learners consider how they will approach a task and take account of their own habits, preferences, strengths and weaknesses. Equally they use their knowledge of the habits, preferences, strengths and weaknesses of their teams to plan and delegate tasks effectively. They are aware of their own and team members' feelings about learning and how to manage them and are aware of a range of personal learning preferences when planning activities and tasks.

Learning Relationships – Leaders who have and make effective learning relationships are able to work independently as well as collaboratively with colleagues. They are open to others' ideas and suggestions and enjoy working with different colleagues to share learning. They are interested in and committed to this learning process and see it as a dynamic one. A leader with this capacity will be a good leader who 'gets the best' out of others and enables colleagues to work effectively within their own preferred mode of working. A leader like this can work flexibly and supportively with others. They seek consensus wherever possible.

Figure 5: Learning/leadership dispositions

Several of these dispositions relate closely to notions of emotional intelligence (Goleman 2002). Headteachers, like other learners, can use self-assessment tools such as the Effective Lifelong Learning Inventory (ELLI) for gaining insights into themselves as learners in order that they can know themselves better and improve their learning as leaders.

We believe that frameworks such as these are helpful for heads in self-evaluating their own work as leaders. However, of more significance to the way in which they behave and lead are the values that underpin their practice – whether these are implicit (as is often the case) or explicit. It is through self-reflection and analysis of their core values that headteachers come to understand their own professional vision and their 'personally-valued competencies'. These may, or may not, be congruent with the publicly assessed and valued knowledge and know-how included in the *National Standards for Headteachers* (DfES 2004).

Headteachers and relationships

It could be said that headteachers are ultimately responsible for modelling and establishing the quality and nature of the learning relationships they wish to characterize in their school community. The most important of these relationships is between students and the professionals who work closest with them and this of course is of critical importance with vulnerable learners (arguably all or most, at some time in their stories). In a piece of empirical research undertaken by one of us, a particular methodology for personalized learning was trialled with a group of 'hard-to-reach' learners, not in employment, education or training, but some of whom were in a young offenders' institution. This methodology, which started with personal choice and used the 'ELLI Dimensions' to scaffold the development of learning power through a six-week personal enquiry project, produced some dramatic improvements in the learning power, confidence and attitudes to the learning of the young participants. One of the key findings concerned the nature of their relationship with the researcher, who adopted the position of a 'learning guide' rather than teacher. What became clear was that learning and creativity flourish where there is a dynamic adaptability in the balance between freedom and structure (or constraint). The scaffolding of learning, through structure, guidance and rules, needed to be stretched or tightened or even removed altogether sometimes, in response to the changing capacity of the learners to grow in confidence, responsibility and autonomy. This required the 'learning guide' to know and observe these changing personal needs and dispositions acutely and, most importantly, to be primarily committed 'to the life narratives of the learners', rather than to a set of learning objectives devised on their behalf (Milner 2006).

What this means, in turn, is that headteachers need to recruit people to their staff who are capable of relating to young people in this way. Just as the hardest part of distributing leadership for some heads may be the letting go of power or control, so the most difficult thing about personalizing learning for many teachers will be the opening up of learning boundaries and continual review of the balance between structure and freedom for each individual learner, in the context of an effective, trusting relationship. The equivalent task for the head is to manage the dynamic tension between the desire to confer and support autonomy on one hand, and the moral imperative to require professionals responsible for leading learning to grow (and even change) in their capacity to meet these demands of personalization on the other hand. This is what we mean by suggesting that there is a single 'continuum' linking personalized learning with distributed leadership: some of the same key themes are apparent, whether we are thinking about our responsibility for managing one's own learning and growth, or the learning of a group of young people, or the vision, improvement and possible transformation of a school. Just as the 'learning guide' needs to be committed to the 'life narratives' of the learners, so a head will need to be committed to the 'life narrative of the school and its wider community'.

Successful headteachers are good at their own relationships (within and outside the school) and good at creating the conditions for effective learning relationships to grow and flourish.

Headteachers' contributions to school ethos and culture

Research suggests, unsurprisingly, that school cultures most conducive to distributed leadership are those that are fully collaborative. Headteachers, in many ways, hold the key to unlocking such cultures. They are the ones who create the opportunities for colleagues to work together. It is through their example that strong personal and professional relationships can be developed. They can help foster commonly held social and moral intentions. In fully collaborative cultures, failures and uncertainty are not protected and defended but shared and discussed – again heads can model this and facilitate the discussion. Finally they can seek to ensure that individuals and groups are simultaneously and inherently valued. In the first case study below we see an example of a head committed to and creating such a culture.

Heads can, in some situations, and with the best intentions, end up creating or supporting less effective cultures, which Day et al. (2003) refer to as 'cultures of connection'. These can be described as 'balkanization' (where separate and competing groups work against each other's interests), 'comfortable collaboration' (where everyone gets on and is involved but there is a lack of reflection and critical self-evaluation) or 'contrived collegiality' (where all the systems and paperwork are in place but there is little ownership or empowerment). Successful heads are aware of the limitations of such cultures and aim for the 'culture of integration' discussed as 'fully collaborative' above.

Another dimension of ethos and culture that are important for both distributed leadership and personalizing learning is learning centredness, introduced in Chapter 2. Here the head recognizes the importance of role modelling, dialogue and monitoring.

School ethos and climate is also related to approaches to behaviour management as these impact directly on learning. Personalized learning is an unobtainable goal if the school cannot sort out pupil behaviour. Small (2006) offers a useful disciplinary taxonomy to help heads and teachers understand the journey towards effective behaviour management. He offers a typology of discipline often found in schools, ranging from despotic at the most extreme and externalized end of the spectrum, to self-discipline at the other end, which comes from within and is therefore more likely to be self-perpetuating and less likely to be dependent.

Discipline type:	Driven by:	Requiring behaviour that is:	Reinforced by:
Despotic	Fear	Cowed	Orders, threats, reprisals
Military	Authority	Compliant/ obedient	Commands, instruction, correction
Organizational	Need for order	Cooperative	Requests, sanctions, explanation, recognition

Discipline type:	Driven by:	Requiring behaviour that is:	Reinforced by:
Functional	Desire for accomplishment	Collaborative	Coaching, praise, success
Self-discipline	Quest for fulfilment/true identity	Consistent/reflective	Modelling, mutual respect, self-value, love

Figure 6: Typology of discipline types

It is our contention that the kinds of discipline towards the 'bottom' of the typology – functional discipline arising out of an activity to be 'mastered', of which learning is a good example, and self-discipline, arising from the desire for self-actualization – are more self-sustaining and less dependent on application by those in authority. When under threat, individuals and organizations understandably tend to resort to the types of discipline nearer the top of the scale, which risks initiating a spiral of decline as discipline becomes more and more dependent upon power and intervention from above. The kinds of behaviour management often refer to as 'firefighting' can sometimes be a symptom, or 'warning bells', of such a decline.

What the leader of a learning organization seeks, for all, is the development of personal power, rather than institutional power. By this, we mean that the power to learn comes from within, from the drive to 'become more fully who we really are' and that it is also this kind of power that persuades others to accept our influence and our leadership. Institutional power, which invokes legal, constitutional or functional authority, such as the power to administer exclusion or require silence in an exam or fire practice, is sometimes essential, but carries with it the risk of increasing dependency, especially when overused or abused.

In the contribution heads make to fostering appropriate culture, ethos and climate, we see both personal and institutional power operating again. The head who seeks to influence through personal rather than institutional power is, in our view, more likely to create sustainable change.

Headteachers as gatekeepers to personalizing learning

If we revisit the gateways to personalizing learning that Hargreaves suggested and which we discussed in Chapter 2, we can see each of these is influenced by the role of the head. In that sense, the head becomes the gatekeeper, although we would argue, in promoting distributed leadership, the head is merely opening some of these gates and allowing others to lead the journey down particular pathways:

- curriculum
- assessment for learning
- learning how to learn

- new technologies for learning
- workforce development
- mentoring and coaching
- school design and organization
- student voice.

Within each of these areas, and others, headteachers find themselves dealing with the complexity and tension between innovation and continuity. There are other creative tensions to manage, too. We have noted the suggestion of Ronnie Woods that an enchanted head might see him or herself as nothing special, but we also know that he or she will adopt a figurehead role when it is called for and accept being looked up to by staff and students alike. It is most often around power issues that tensions are found. The extent to which these tensions end up being creative, leading to innovative ideas and developments which benefit young people, will often depend upon a headteacher's ability to hold things in tension which could, if allowed to, become polarizing ideas and tendencies. For instance, nothing symbolizes the head's position as gatekeeper more tangibly than the power to exclude a student. The weighing of the interests of an individual against those of the wider community – which have been threatened by the attitude or behaviour of the individual – is among the most challenging judgements required by a school leader. A head who can turn such moments into opportunities for articulating the moral dilemma, inviting others to join in holding the tension before rushing to judgement, is modelling moral courage and developing leadership capacity in the wider team.

The following case studies explore how two headteachers, one from a primary school and one from a secondary school, have set about opening all of the gateways and managing the creative tensions involved in innovations designed to give young people a genuinely personalized experience of learning.

Case Study 1

Waycroft Primary School

Waycroft is an example of a school where distributed leadership and personalizing learning have been the goal for some time and where the results of that synergy are exemplified. When Ofsted inspected Waycroft in 2007 the outcome was extraordinary – the school was described as 'remarkable in every respect' (Ofsted 2007). The word 'outstanding' was used 15 times in the five-page report and was the rating given for all 27 criteria used in the inspection. According to the report, the school 'exemplifies all that is best in primary education'. With regard to leadership and the extent to which it is distributed, the inspector described it as outstanding from 'top to bottom', which implies a hierarchical structure that does not in reality exist. The headteacher 'ensures that everyone has the opportunity, self-confidence and support to make a positive contribution to the management (sic) of the school, and is very good at getting the best out of all his colleagues'.

Case Study 1, *cont.*

The achievements of the pupils, who come from 'mid-twentieth-century housing estates', are 'exceptionally high' and their 'outstanding personal development and well-being are a tribute to the high priority the school gives to this area'. 'Pupils develop a wonderful love of learning...and are developing an outstanding sense of being good citizens and contributing to community life.'

Simon Rowe has been headteacher at Waycroft Primary School in Bristol for eight years. Waycroft was formed from the amalgamation of separate infant and junior schools when he took over. It currently has approximately 450 pupils in 14 classes and a nursery. The school is successful in terms of its results (within the top 5 per cent) but is in an area where some parents, according to Simon, tend not to value lifelong learning and have low aspirations for their offspring.

He is a committed and enthusiastic school leader who welcomes visitors and enjoys the opportunity to talk about his values, the school's achievements and the challenges he faces. He constantly refers to the extent to which everyone is valued in his school and reinforces any success as being the success of all, not that of individuals.

Simon's learning journey as a school leader involved previous headships in small rural schools and that has had significant influence on his approach to personalizing learning. He has sought, in his words, 'to develop a "small school ethos" in the larger school setting of Waycroft'. This included his aspiration for pupils to be known well by teachers and other staff so that their individual needs can be fully understood and addressed – so ensuring that their learning can be personalized.

The success of distributed leadership at Waycroft is underpinned by the professional relationship that Simon has established and that exists among all staff as a result of his influence. He values those relationships and invests time and energy in them as is evident to anyone who has the opportunity to be shown around the school.

Additionally, the school's structure and organization are set up to support distributed leadership. There are two tiers of formal structure – tier one is the head, deputy and assistant head. Tier two involves eight other team leaders (Foundation, Key Stage 1, Lower Key Stage 2, Upper Key Stage 2, Special Educational Needs Coordinator (SENCO) and core Subject Leaders) who have responsibilities that include performance management of staff. Tier one meets every Friday afternoon to review the week and plan for the next, including Monday's staff meeting. Tier two meets formally approximately six times a year. Team leaders are explicitly encouraged to provide leadership opportunities for others to take a lead on particular areas or at particular times (for example, a Newly Qualified Teacher took responsibility for an INSET day that focused on ensuring that design and technology addressed children's experience and interests, which led to a revision of the design and technology scheme of work). So, although a hierarchical organization is evident, the staff feel empowered and valued, which motivates them to take up opportunities available. Non-teaching staff are equally valued at Waycroft and the impact of distributed leadership is evident in their activities – for example, lunchtime supervisors are in teams with 'play leaders'. Simon regards the organization of the school

Case Study 1, *cont.*

office as another essential part of effective school operation – he sees the efficiency of that allowing him more time to concentrate on his leadership role.

Another of Simon's key drivers has been the need for consistency across the school which, for him, is fostered by shared leadership: policies are developed by teams and negotiated, so staff are clear about what should happen, and then everyone is encouraged to take shared responsibility for making it happen. This involves all adults taking responsibility for consistency with all learners – in the classroom and beyond. This was particularly important after the amalgamation and according to Ofsted has become 'a strength' of the school.

Celebrating achievement is important at Waycroft and there is an explicit 'responding to children's work' policy that covers the whole continuum from 'smiles' to formal prizes (including lots of trophies for various areas, both academic and non-academic). The policy supports the school's desire to develop further their approaches to 'assessment for learning'. This has led to what Ofsted described as 'exemplary marking, assessment and target setting'. The use of assessment data is another dimension of this. The school aims for a minimum of two-thirds of a National Curriculum level improvement for each pupil every year. There is a sophisticated tracking system in place to identify pupils at risk of not reaching their targets. This system is the responsibility of the deputy head who has an assessment brief. She liaises with the SENCO to plan specific intervention strategies for specific pupils. This is another way, according to Simon, of applying the small school ethos in a systematic way, as it involves good management (for example, the tracking system) as well as good leadership (vision and strategic thinking). Behaviour is also monitored systematically and this is something that involves all adults (including the large teams of lunchtime supervisors and teaching assistants) using a simple pro forma. In a large primary school, a pupil could be interacting with five or six adults in the school day and the tracking system aims to ensure a good flow of communication. The approach to behaviour is based on 'golden rules' and these rules form the basis of the tracking. Simon analyses the outcomes of this process every Friday and follows up with parents and class teachers any concerns where children's behaviours are acting as blocks to their learning. However, the overall success of this is not just a result of the systems being in place: the key to the success of the systems is, once again, the quality of relationships. Simon's relationships with young people – as with staff – lead to them feeling personally valued and motivated to improve. Again, it is 'personal power' working in tandem with 'institutional power' that makes the difference here.

Another gateway to personalized learning, learning to learn, has been a focus of recent developments at the school. They have introduced 'Building Learning Power' (BLP) (Claxton 2002) through a staff development programme (led by tier one). This is an early formulation taken from the research that ultimately led to the ELLI learning power dimensions. According to Simon, it is now being consistently used across the school. In particular, the language of learning associated with BLP permeates various aspects of the school's work. It forms the basis, for example, of the reward system, planning and monitoring of lessons, online quizzes and so on. Simon has been careful to use the language of learning accurately and consistently in assemblies and other contexts to provide a role model for staff and pupils. Teachers were supported through INSET activities in understanding their coaching role with pupils and used case studies from other schools to discuss and develop their understanding of issues related to changing practice to make them more learning centred. Simon now finds parents, as well as staff and pupils, talking the same learning language. According to Simon, this has helped parents understand and value learning more. At the foundation stage, pictures have been used to make the 'language' accessible. Super heroes or characters to support children's understanding such as 'Resili Ant' (Resilience) and 'Mr Mirror' (Reflectiveness) have been created and modelled to help children 'image' some of the 'learning muscles' that they are developing. Ofsted saw the results and described the pupils' 'wonderful love for learning'. By Year 6 they 'know in detail what they have to do to learn best in any situation'.

To further raise pupil and parent aspirations, the school promotes the previous achievement of ex-pupils through displays and local media coverage.

Simon considers professional relationships within the school to be good. The staffing situation is very stable and there is little turnover. Many teachers have had differing responsibilities over the time they have been at Waycroft and succession planning and retention are seen as important and fostered by giving colleagues a variety of challenges and responsibility. Subject leaders have opportunities for classroom observations of colleagues that have coaching dimensions – observations have a focus (perhaps on an aspect of learning) and feedback is offered in ways that are intended to be formative and lead to further development. A standard feedback pro forma is used to allow Simon to monitor all such observations. Performance management is not seen as 'threatening' at Waycroft, as staff, according to Simon, welcome the opportunities involved in such monitoring. He considers the school to have a culture of openness in which professional dialogue is common and valued.

Subject leadership was identified by Ofsted in 2002 as in need of further development. Subject leaders now have clear guidance on the nature of their roles and tasks they should be completing including: lesson observations; long-term planning; pupil conferencing (subject leaders meet with a small group of pupils); presentations to governors; SAT analysis; policy update. Evidence files are compiled to support the school self-evaluation form (SEF) and Ofsted inspections. These proved their worth in the recent inspection.

Personalizing learning through curriculum approaches at Waycroft pre-dates the national driver for personalized learning. A broad and balanced curriculum that engages all pupils has been Simon's goal since he arrived at Waycroft. He claims they have never placed undue focus on the core subjects at the expense of time given to foundation subjects. As an ex-PE teacher he believes that pupil engagement results from a varied and flexible curriculum. He has sought to appoint staff who are good classroom teachers and who have wide ranging interests. He encourages them to take risks in their planning and teaching and sees evidence of this in enriching pupils' learning experiences. There are several musicians, sports enthusiasts and creative artists on the staff. He has never encouraged 'cramming for SATs' and says that, even in the run-up to SATs, Year 6

Case Study 1, *cont.*

students are being offered a broad curriculum in which creativity and enjoyment is valued. He is keen to ensure children want to come to school and that the school provides them with broad experiences to engage them – whether these are traditional lessons or extra-curricular activities. The school's planning is available on the school intranet system to foster improved subject links – subject leaders can easily access planning in other subjects to ensure continuity and progression. The school has always organized cross-curricula and specialist weeks such as an 'international week' or 'science week' during which the whole school engages with the particular theme in place of the traditional curriculum. These events provide opportunities for pupils to pursue activities that particularly interest them and opportunities for more pupil-directed and independent learning. Ofsted reported that it is 'an exceptionally high quality curriculum which grabs the imagination of all pupils'.

Simon and his colleagues work hard at addressing pupils' special educational needs, through schemes such as Reading Recovery (the SENCO is an expert in this), which has been well established at Waycroft for eight years. Ofsted said 'outstanding progress was made by pupils with learning difficulties'. Reading Recovery work is now supported with funding from a KPMG grant. He sees approaches such as this benefiting all pupils in an inclusive way as they influence the quality of teaching in ways that go beyond the support offered for individual pupils by the SENCO. Simon's own learning through international links was significant in this area since he saw good use being made of Reading Recovery on a British Council funded visit to New Zealand some years ago.

Another of Hargreaves' personalized learning gateways, 'student voice', is evident at Waycroft. There is a well-established school council which addresses learning issues as well as others – for example, the development of Building Learning Power was discussed with them at the planning stage and they are used to monitor how new developments are going. Personalized learning is also enhanced by the house system – there are four houses with house captains and vice-captains which offers another 'home' for pupils and provides other ways to support the 'small school ethos' in which pupils feel known and valued. There are house assemblies (for KS1 and KS2) that are relatively small meetings and organized as circle times. Simon will often encourage all pupils to talk to house captains about the issues he raises if they would like to give feedback to him or other staff concerns that they have. Again, personal relationships and dialogue are crucial – the existence of the systems alone is not enough.

Learning is supported through extensive use of new technologies – there are two laptop suites, a PC suite as well as PCs and internet connections in all classes. An Information and Communications Technology (ICT) specialist teaches all classes twice a week and makes sure every pupil works individually (as opposed to working in a pair or group) at least once every three weeks in these specialist lessons. This was introduced when it became clear some pupils were avoiding keyboard activity and not developing appropriate skills through group or paired work. There are other ICT opportunities offered – for example, a specific government-funded 'girls-focused' ICT group. The school employs a part-time technician to support ICT work.

Case Study 1, *cont.*

Another approach to fostering more personalized learning at Waycroft has involved the extensive development of the library as a learning resource area – Simon's thinking with regard to this was influenced by a trip he took to look at schools in Denver. Waycroft employs a part-time, enthusiastic, librarian who has helped turn the library area into a stimulating space that children are encouraged to use and which fosters their independence and engagement with texts. ICT is an important part of the centre. The use of resources is monitored electronically so that the school can analyse, for example, what Year 6 boys are accessing (currently and interestingly, more books than Year 6 girls).

Simon's 'worry list' is currently dominated by issues related to 'parenting' and the school's role in the community in the context of *Every Child Matters* and *Extended Schools*. He worries that schools are being asked to do too much and that there are a small minority of parents in each class who are reluctant to engage constructively with the school. Schools cannot succeed in isolation and parental responsibility cannot be absolved and given to schools. He is keen to engage with parents more regularly and new facilities are being developed to move this forward.

Case Study 2

St John's School and Community College

Patrick Hazlewood has been head of St John's Marlborough since 1996. It is his second headship. Since 1999, he has worked with the RSA – Royal Society for the encouragement of Arts, Manufactures and Commerce – on the 'Opening Minds' curriculum project – 'Education for the 21st Century' – which 'places the learner at the centre of educational endeavour and redefines the role of the teacher'.

St John's is – and has been for a long time – a large, happy, successful secondary school with a growing sixth form and a good reputation in its community: a rural market town and outlying villages set in countryside of outstanding natural beauty.

In 2000, the school was judged by Ofsted to be 'very effective'. For Patrick, all the positive feedback from this was counterbalanced by the first stirrings of concern. He saw that the school was achieving success largely through the overworking of staff and the compliance of children. A plateau had been reached. Performance, on this basis, would be hard to sustain and could only really go down. It was time for radical reform.

Case Study 2, *cont.*

The reforms at St John's have attracted widespread attention since then, not because they offer a recipe for success, but because they tell a story about what it means and costs to have a vision of education for the time we live in, to ask some of the hard questions raised by it and to set about making it a reality.

The vision, in a nutshell, sounds like this. It is Patrick's view that, through no fault of their own, schools began to get things badly wrong during the 1990s. There was a lack of deep and rigorous thought about what they were actually for. There was an expansion of the powers of such agencies as examination boards, the Qualifications and Curriculum Authority (QCA), the Specialist Colleges Trust, all stimulating initiatives and developing a culture of accountability. However much we might agree with their ultimate goal, this ended up creating a 'concentricity of busyness', when what was needed was the space for creative people to ask 'What really matters here?' For Patrick, what really mattered was acknowledging and upholding each child's responsibility for accessing the learning from which they could most benefit. No one else has the divine right to say what that child's curriculum should consist of. 'Every day that a child spends with us, matters. We cannot afford to debilitate her learning capacity, ever! There will always be different views of what is right for her, so the answer is to put her at the centre and ask her to take real, active responsibility for taking her learning forward.'

What flowed from this learner-centred philosophy amounts to a radical redesign of a learning organization. The management structures had already been changed to underline the concept of collegiality, based on the understanding that the most important relationships in the school were those between teacher and child. The collegial theme was strengthened by all staff, including support staff, being involved in a series of twilight seminars through which the hard questions were addressed together, about the nature of a curriculum for the twenty-first century and how it could be implemented. The shift in ethos improved students' attitudes, results and the receptiveness of everyone to change. In 2001 the 'Integrated Curriculum' was introduced into Year 7 as a pilot project. In 2003 it ceased to be a pilot and was called 'The Alternative Curriculum' and by 2005 it was subsumed into the school's Key Stage 3 curriculum model.

There is not the space here to describe the new curriculum in detail (a full account can be found in Bosher and Hazlewood 2005) but it is worth describing some key features. It was designed around six 'competencies' needed for survival and success:

- numeracy and problem solving
- literacy and communication
- organizing information
- organizing self and relating to people
- citizenship
- emotional intelligence and empathy.

These formed the framework for the self-assessment, monitoring and review of progress.

Case Study 2, *cont.*

It was clear that this thinking was cutting across subject boundaries, so two more radical changes followed to the way the curriculum was organized: first, it was delivered to each Year 7 teaching group by a team of six teachers, who needed to develop the confidence and expertise to work outside their own specialized areas; second, the content was accessed through six modules in a year, with broad thematic titles, such as:

- being unique
- higher, faster, stronger
- making the news
- going places
- forests
- counting the cost.

These changes achieved two things very quickly: first, they improved relationships, since teachers and students saw more of each other each week; second, they freed the students, themselves working in small teams, to make decisions and choices about where their learning should lead. The changes also required two things quickly: first, teachers to welcome a steep learning curve in their own professional development and second, a 'mapping exercise', to monitor what was learned against the requirements of the National Curriculum, on which the students would of course be formally tested at the end of the key stage.

In time, the early dramatic improvements in students' attitudes, motivation and behaviour were translated into a reduction of the Key Stage 3 curriculum to two years instead of three, since so much more ground was covered in the given time. Almost all the conventional measures of performance went up significantly.

How does this relate to our key themes of 'personalized learning' and 'distributed leadership'? The extent to which learning was more 'personal' to each learner seems fairly self-evident in both the philosophy and practice of the new curriculum at St John's. Importantly, it is *not* seen as the school and its teachers personalizing learning *on behalf of* the students; it is about releasing the energy and developing the responsibility of the students to personalize it *for themselves*.

The distribution of leadership is clearly a key factor in Patrick's vision and the way in which the reforms have taken root at the school. It was clear to him from the start that teachers would need to be 'taken into' the business of change and that both groups (those established in 'old ways' and those more recently trained, simply to organize and deliver the National Curriculum), might struggle. He wanted a staff of independent professionals who see no limits to what they could achieve with their students. That was another reason for creating teams of six – to support the professionalism and development of each. He was influenced by the notions of 'extended professionalism', developed by Michael Fullan (1988) and Linda Darling-Hammond (1990; 1994), through which teachers are seen as capable of taking decisions for themselves: 'Had a good idea? Do it! Don't wait

Case Study 2, *cont.*

until you have been able to ask permission!' Old hierarchical models were replaced by teams of fellow professionals of equal worth, defining together how they would work and collaborate.

The Teaching and Learning Responsibility (TLR) restructuring exercise in 2005–6 offered opportunities for consolidating the principle in a new structure focusing properly on supporting learning. Titles such as head and deputy head of department, serving redundant 'box ticking, accountability' functions, disappeared. They were replaced by leadership dedicated to the professional development of the teams of teachers and to the progress of the students aged from 5 to 19. 'Whole-School Strategy Managers' were made responsible for such things as *Assessment for Learning*, work-related and vocational education and performance data analysis. 'Directors of Impact and Innovation' were appointed, to help teachers to adjust and improve the curriculum (defined as 'everything') by observing and understanding its impact on each child. 'Phase Progression Leaders' were appointed to look in a more longitudinal way at whether students are properly enabled to make seamless, unhindered progress, from age 5 to 13 and from 13 to 19. The overlap (at age 13) means that these leaders have a year of joint responsibility to hand over their personal knowledge, taper the input of one and increase that of the other. The theme is clear again, that both personalized learning and distributed leadership are often more about removing barriers to learning than making new things happen.

Patrick would say it is also an essential part of the sustainability of the vision to have what he calls 'an organic understanding of the organization', in which roles and structures are fluid and responsive to change, the rigid assumptions and power differentials of old hierarchical models are left behind. The extent of this commitment to fluidity and continual evolution is evident in the redesign of the whole school's curriculum structure over the last 18 months. Instead of the traditional subject departments and faculty structure, there are now four 'schools', all focused on the education of human beings in the global dimension of the twenty-first century:

- School of Human Exploration
- School of Human Communication
- School of Human Enterprise
- School of Human Performance.

Although this raised eyebrows when it was first proposed, in a mere 18 months it has become part of the way people think about the organization of learning in the school.

The next step in this story of 'evolutionary adaptation' to the times we live in and to the learners 'who are at the heart of everything we do', is what Patrick calls 'Radical Collegiality': embracing students into the 'collegial responsibility of the organization' as co-researchers, observers, and participants, 'co-constructing the pedagogy', having equal worth and therefore an equal voice. A small group, consisting of a dozen students in each of the three year groups, 8, 9 and 10, are already being trained as researchers, together with partners from a school in Essex. They will train and teach the others. 'If you teach something, you know it better yourself,' says Patrick. 'You enquire into the learning

Case Study 2, *cont.*

environment and understand the frustrations...' The idea is to give students some of the 'expert status' once reserved for teachers.

Of course, it has not all been plain sailing. Change does bring confusion, frustration, even panic at times. Patrick explains what happened when panic set in, in the autumn of 2006. An independent evaluation exercise revealed general enthusiasm for the philosophy of the curriculum reforms (which Patrick describes as 'common sense and difficult to argue against') but equally widespread concern about how to implement them. People were saying 'I don't know what to do!' and instead of being given a script or an answer were asked to go away and 'Think about it!' What happened next was a good illustration of the ultimate benefits of distributed leadership, which had to include a determined letting go of the power and control that the head was being invited – almost implored – to take back. The 'Phase Progression Coordinators' began to meet of their own accord and started to come up with solutions. Instead of the Leadership Team writing a School Development Plan, teams were beginning to draft their own strategic plans and circulate them for consultation. It was beginning to take off!

In summing up the vision, Patrick would come back to the kind of students he wants the school to produce: confident, capable, competent learners who know how to go about learning, also to interrogate and challenge their environment. He wants to 'put challenge at every level in the organization', so *anyone* can challenge the status quo. He wants the organic growth of the school community to lead, naturally, from the *integrated curriculum* into the *integration of leadership and learning*.

As for the evolution of his own role, he believes there will always be a need for a head, not to tell people 'how it is' or what to do, but to understand, represent and speak on behalf of the community and all its members. He acknowledges that a certain kind of ruthlessness was and is necessary on his part, to be so uncompromising about the vision and need for reform. Now, he has come to a point in his own learning journey when his leadership is about trying to be 'the reflective voice', recognizing the fallibility and vulnerability of human beings – especially teachers, who are so naturally self-critical and who need their 'souls and spirits' to become more robust. He believes their growth is better served by him acting as 'an understanding listener' than 'a leader so full of himself that he knows exactly what they should do!'

Conclusion

This chapter has addressed the opportunities and challenges that distributing leadership offers headteachers. To let go and allow others to take on leadership responsibilities is not easy and requires qualities more associated with relational learning, as opposed to those associated with the heroic head leading from the front. The headteacher who is successful in establishing a culture conducive to distributed leadership will be part of a learning community in which the relationship between student, staff and organizational learning works in an iterative way that is mutually supportive and beneficial. Archbishop Desmond Tutu (2000) captures the interdependency between self and community well in his description of the Zulu concept 'Ubuntu'. He says, 'A person with Ubuntu is open and available to others, affirming of others, does not feel threatened that others are able and good, for he or she has a proper self-assurance that comes from knowing that he or she belongs in a greater whole,' in essence 'a person is a person through others.'

In the next chapter, we look at the ways in which middle and subject leaders in schools can enhance their impact on personalizing learning if their leadership potential is released by their headteachers.

Chapter 6

Releasing leadership potential: the role of middle leaders and subject leaders in personalizing learning

Introduction

Distributed leadership, as we have seen, extends the boundaries of leadership to others in the school beyond the headteacher as designated leader. An obvious group of teachers who are likely to be part of that extended group in most schools are those who are already regarded as middle leaders – usually teachers who are primarily classroom-based, but who are given roles and responsibilities that extend beyond their classrooms and, sometimes, across the whole school.

This chapter explores the nature of middle leadership in the context of distributed leadership and, in particular, it focuses on the role of subject leaders or those involved in subject leadership as part of the school's learning and teaching strategy. This group, it can be argued, is key to successfully personalizing learning for young people since learning occurs throughout the curriculum, which in England is framed by the subjects of the National Curriculum, even in schools that seek to operate a more integrated curriculum. While headteachers, as discussed in the last chapter, are effectively the gatekeepers with regard to the routes to personalizing learning, such as curriculum change, it is subject leaders and teachers who make things happen. We will consider the roles of subject leaders or heads of department (in secondary schools) and the opportunities and challenges involved. These are adults in schools with a leadership role through title, designation or responsibility. A later chapter will address the contribution of teachers without formally designated roles to a school's leadership capacity.

The process of personalizing learning for young people is essentially a process of change that requires leading and managing, as we have discussed in previous chapters. This chapter will examine the contribution of middle leaders to this process and consider the extent to which they can be regarded as agents of change. It will explore their learning journeys; the qualities, values and dispositions involved; and reinforce the significance of the personal and the importance of relationships.

Case studies will be used to provide insights into the processes of school improvement aimed at enhancing schools' capacity to personalize learning for young people and the degree to which we see some of the parallels between distributing leadership and personalizing learning discussed in Chapter 4.

Middle leadership

Before considering who are the designated middle leaders in schools, we should recognize a tension between the hierarchical nature of school organization suggested by the label 'middle leadership' and the aspiration of distributing leadership to play down the significance of hierarchy and empower others through increasing their professional responsibility and decision making. We will see in later case studies that schools with hierarchical structures illustrate that the tension can be resolved.

So, who are these middle leaders? They function in a number of designated roles within schools. Whether deputy or assistant heads in schools should be considered middle leaders is, however, a moot point. For our purposes, we include them, although some might argue these roles usually have much more to do with management than leadership. In our experience, schools where distributed leadership is evident are schools where assistant and deputy heads' roles are ones where leadership is recognized as a significant part of the roles.

Some of the roles we would include in the middle leadership group often carry a title such as coordinator that, to some extent, disguises the leadership dimension of the role(s). A staff development coordinator or Special Educational Needs Coordinator (SENCO) are two such examples. In these cases, although administrative and management activities may dominate the post holders' activities, there is significant potential in schools where distributed leadership is encouraged for these post holders to contribute to leadership. Indeed, the SENCO potentially has a key contribution to make to schools' aspirations to extend the personalized dimension of learning for particular pupils and, in schools recognizing the benefits of inclusivity, their work can impact positively on the approaches to learning and teaching of all pupils, as noted in the case study of Waycroft Primary School in the last chapter.

Most schools have designated year or phase leaders (again, sometimes labelled coordinators). In primary schools, there is usually someone designated to lead the Early Years or Foundation stage. Secondary schools in England have strategy managers and year team leaders or other year leaders or key stage leaders of some description with a pastoral role. Another group of teachers who are potentially middle leaders are those given responsibilities for themes or strands – for example 'citizenship' or 'international links'.

However, we intend to focus our consideration in this chapter on subject leaders or those with a key responsibility for learning and teaching. These are often heads of department or strategy leaders in secondary schools, where they may get significant timetable relief for the role. In primary schools, subject leaders or teaching and learning leaders are, in most cases, classroom teachers who get little, if any, time allocated to the role. We say 'in most cases' since it is not uncommon for headteachers in primary schools to also take on a subject responsibility or two or lead on teaching and learning. We also acknowledge that in some primary schools subject leadership is allocated to pairs of teachers (perhaps experienced and less experienced colleagues or someone from each key stage) or small teams.

In some primary schools, the labels for subject leaders can also be misleading in that the term 'subject coordinator' or 'manager' is still used. In these schools, the leadership dimension of the role is sometimes minimal and, perhaps, not even recognized. Differences between subject leadership and coordination are discussed in detail by one of us elsewhere (Bell and Ritchie 1999).

We consider there to be a key leadership role associated with subjects in schools, even in contexts where, for example in primary, the curriculum is planned and implemented in a way that integrates rather than fragments it into subjects.

What do we know about the roles of subject leaders?

Bennett et al. (2003b) provide a comprehensive review of the literature related to subject leadership. We begin our exploration with a reminder that there are National Standards for Subject Leaders (TTA 1998) that, although now somewhat dated, set out a framework that provides the 'publicly valued qualities, knowledge and know-how'. These standards outline:

- core purpose of subject leadership
- key outcomes of subject leadership
- professional knowledge and understanding
- skills and attributes
- key areas of subject leadership.

The core purpose was 'to provide professional leadership for the subject to secure high-quality teaching and effective use of resources to ensure improved standards of achievement for all pupils'.

In the context of this book, we would reword this as 'to provide professional leadership for the subject to secure high-quality teaching and effective use of resources to ensure personalized learning for all pupils that leads to improved standards of achievement and well-being'. The outcomes related to *Every Child Matters* (DfES 2003) require schools to aspire to more than merely achievement.

The standards described the knowledge and understanding, skills and qualities required of effective subject leaders:

- Knowledge and understanding – subject; pedagogy; curriculum.
- Skills – leadership skills; decision-making skills; communication skills; self-management skills.
- Attributes – self-confidence; adaptability; energy; perseverance; reliability; enthusiasm; and integrity.

The standards outline the role of subject leaders in four areas: Strategic Direction and Development; Teaching and Learning; Leading and Managing Staff; Effective and Efficient Deployment of Staff and Resources.

One of us has written elsewhere about the implementation of these standards in primary schools (Bell and Ritchie 1999; Ritchie 2006).

A more current articulation of the role of subject leadership in secondary schools is available in the Secondary National Strategy materials for KS3. In 2002 the DfES published *Securing Improvement: the role of subject leaders* (see www.standards.dfes. gov.uk/keystage3). This identified three core roles for subject leaders: judging standards; evaluating teaching and learning; and leading sustainable improvement. In other words, it prioritized a sub-set of the role first set out in the National Standards.

It stresses the need for subject leaders to make secure judgements about the standards of pupils' attainment, rate of progress and personal development on the basis of evidence. This involves analysing and interpreting assessment data. They are expected to understand what makes teaching effective in their subjects and are seen as accountable for the quality of teaching in 'their' subjects. They should be systematically observing colleagues teaching and providing constructive and objective feedback. They are expected to be confident in their role as leaders of teachers and other adults in their teams. This involves inspiring and enthusing others as they create the capacity for change. Subject leaders, the document states, should encourage others to review and improve their practice and ensure changes are 'embedded in the subject team's practice' (DfES 2002: 3).

The document outlines expectations of strategy managers and year team leaders. The nature of specific tasks involved for all three roles is also detailed and provides an audit tool for subject leaders to evaluate their current practice.

Subject leaders' learning journeys and learning selves

Regardless of what is documented about the publicly valued competencies related to subject leadership, the success of subject leaders in supporting personalizing learning in schools is essentially a result of their particular learning journeys as they develop as teachers and as leaders. Middle leaders' routes to leadership are stories of personal growth and, using an ecological metaphor, such growth needs to occur in contexts where the conditions are conducive to growth – conditions often created by the headteacher. Subject leaders' personal values, qualities and attitudes result from many factors, including their educational histories, their experience as teachers in the classroom and their experience as followers of leaders for whom they have worked. Bennis (1989) refers to becoming a leader as a process of self-invention and regards becoming a leader as synonymous with becoming an authentic person. Like effective headteachers, effective middle leaders need to view themselves as learners and role models to others – they need their leadership to be built on personal authenticity. Their authenticity, as West-Burnham (2004) reminds us, is a result of the interaction between 'values, language and capacity to act'. Gaining such authenticity as a leader takes time and is undoubtedly a complex journey. It is a process of 'becoming' rather than the development of a particular set of competencies.

In supporting other teachers in making change subject leaders have advantages over headteachers in that they can role model good classroom practice in ways that are more difficult for headteachers. They can demonstrate to others how they seek to 'live out their values in practice'; how difficult that can be; and how accepting criticism can often be a route to more fully living out those values. We will see, in the first case study below, a good example of how a subject leader used her own practice as a model for whole-school practice aimed at enhancing personalized learning. In this and other examples in this book, we see middle leaders who hold strongly-held values regarding learning and teaching that are drivers for their own practice and for the way they seek to influence the practice of others and whole-school approaches. Successful subject leaders need credibility among colleagues as effective teachers, especially in their specialist subject, and as practitioners who recognize they are on a continuing learning journey themselves. They are unlikely to be leaders who prioritize telling others how to do it, or indeed just showing others through their own example. They are more likely to work collaboratively with others – working with colleagues in a 'let's enquire together' mode to improve things. They are leaders who can demonstrate, through their own practice, how the gateways to personalizing learning can be opened in the classroom, whether that gateway relates to supporting learners in learning to learn, assessment for learning, providing flexible approaches to the curriculum, or valuing and working with student voice.

Leadership cannot happen in isolation – it is a social act and middle leaders need to be open and available to others and see themselves as authentic leaders and human beings through their relationships with others. Middle leaders are in a complex set of relationships in which they, like headteachers, need to develop their 'Ubuntu' (see Chapter 5) as leaders.

Clearly, subject leaders' professional relationships with colleagues, as peers, are somewhat different from the professional relationships that a headteacher can establish. However, as we discussed in the previous chapters, forming strong, trusting, professional relationships is essential to successful leadership. Leaders need to understand themselves in relation to others, it's part of their emotional intelligence. It can be difficult, especially in a small school, for a subject leader to move beyond cultures of 'comfortable collaboration' (Day et al. 1993) and engage in relationships in which they feel able to engage constructively with colleagues and deal with issues related to learning and teaching that need addressing. Sometimes that means asking challenging questions and moving colleagues out of comfort zones, for example, in the context of a coaching relationship or as a result of classroom monitoring. Sometimes, it means that they have to move outside their own comfort zones as they learn from feedback from others and from experience. Subject leaders need to work well in teams and to know themselves as team players. Inevitably, given the nature of the role and the primacy of their teaching roles, subject leaders and other leaders will at different times be followers, leaders and team members. These contributions require different skills and qualities but in all integrity and living out one's values are necessary.

Subject leaders' learning journeys as leaders can be usefully informed by the leadership frameworks introduced in Chapters 3 and 5, adapted to acknowledge the constraints on their leadership activities given the primacy of their teaching role. The learning/leadership dispositions introduced in Chapters 2 and 5 provide a tool for middle leaders to self-assess their own learning and leadership capacity.

Challenges facing subject leaders

In a previous publication, one of us (Ritchie 2006: 14–15) identified a number of key challenges faced by subject leaders and those who have responsibility for leading teaching and learning more generically as 'leaders of learning' or perhaps as advanced skills teachers in primary schools. We will now revisit some of these challenges and consider the implications for a move towards greater personalization of learning in schools.

The challenges to subject leaders or those involved in subject leadership include:

- Taking up the offer in the policy documents and guidance to become more autonomous.

- Having a vision and engaging in strategic thinking to address the changing policy context.

- Developing the school's pedagogy.

- Developing approaches to coaching that improve the quality of teaching.

- Making the most of assessment data to support individualized target setting and to help the school match teaching to learners' needs.

- Engaging in whole curriculum development.

- Embracing creativity, culture and citizenship.

- Finding creative ways to systematically monitor the quality of teaching and learning.

- Making the most of school self-evaluation as a route to school improvement.

- Focusing on improvement and engaging in collaborative school-based research.

- Developing and sharing practice through networks.

These challenges provide an agenda that is relevant, we would suggest, to primary and secondary phases and, as noted, to those with more generic responsibilities for teaching and learning.

The first challenge relates to a changing policy context in which *Excellence and Enjoyment* (2003), the DfES *Five Year Strategy* (DfES 2004) and other guidance from the DfES, encourages schools to ensure their approaches are adapted to the needs of the learners and the community in which they are located. There are interesting parallels here, as we think about autonomy, with distributed leadership. In Chapter 3, we discussed the significance of individuals and teams considering that they have autonomy, which we understand as the freedom to make professional judgements within the framework of the school's shared vision and mission. There is therefore some congruence with what evidence suggests supports effective distributed leadership and with what the government says it wants. Clearly there are tensions between the government's rhetoric related to autonomy and their accountability agenda and the constraints some may see Ofsted and the inspection regime placing on schools. This may manifest itself as a tension for teachers between their professional values and judgement and the requirements of external accountability.

If subject leaders are going to justify the label 'leaders' then they need to contribute strategically to the school and, crucially, that means having a view of where the subject is going – that is, a vision of a preferred future related to learning and teaching in the subject – whether that is in a separate curriculum area or as part of a more integrated or innovative curriculum. This is the first of the four areas described in the national standards for subject leaders, although given less prominence in the later KS3 materials (DfES 2002). We do not see how a subject leader can be effective without a view of a preferred future. We would encourage such a vision of a subject to encompass the way in which the subject leader's particular subjects will contribute constructively to the move towards more personalizing of learning and, of course, how it needs to be constructed within and congruent with the overall school's mission and vision. In schools where pairs or teams take responsibility for subject leadership, or the approach is based on a broader non-subject specific approach, the need for a vision of a preferred future stands but will need to be co-constructed with others.

Developing a strategic view will, ideally, relate to the challenge of contributing to a school's pedagogy. This is, in some respects, the most important goal for personalizing learning since it embraces all that is needed for such change to result. Pedagogy is a somewhat underused term in this country, although it is much more common in other European countries. It embraces the discourses related to learning, teaching and the curriculum – in other words it brings together what is known about the core business of schools. *Excellence and Enjoyment: a Strategy for Primary Schools* (DfES 2003), provided an opportunity for the government to articulate a national pedagogic statement but some argue it is inadequate in this respect. Robin Alexander, in a thought-provoking article entitled *Still no pedagogy? Principle, pragmatism and compliance in primary education* (2004: 28), provides a strong critique of the document, claiming: 'The Primary Strategy is badly written, poorly argued and deeply patronising in its assumption that teachers will be seduced by Ladybird language, pretty pictures, offers of freedom and enjoyment, and populist appeals to their common sense. There is no case, no argument, some fragments of a strategy, but certainly no vision.'

The knowledge base currently available to the profession, created through research and other means, such as that discussed in Chapter 2, provides a rich resource to inform construction of school-specific pedagogies. This knowledge base is much larger than that previously available to teachers and one of the huge challenges for subject leaders is deciding what of that knowledge base is most useful and relevant to their own situation – what should inform and underpin a school learning and teaching policy and guidance. Interestingly, Alexander is also very critical of the failure of the authors of the Primary Strategy to draw on research, accusing them of 'wilful amnesia' (2004: 6) in this respect. It is also important for subject leaders to engage critically with what others say and write. Critiques of 'good ideas' like learning styles (Coffield et al. 2004) and 'multiple intelligences' (White 2004) need to be given serious consideration before subject leaders (and schools) rush into new approaches.

We will see, through case studies, examples of subject leaders/leaders of teaching and learning contributing constructively to a school's pedagogy and using such pedagogical thinking to improve practice.

Subject leaders cannot operate in isolation and, as we discussed in the previous section, another strand of their role concerns the way in which they work with others, either individually or in teams. Indeed in some schools, the responsibility for a subject, or group of subjects, may be the responsibility of a pair or team. The purpose of collaboration between subject leaders and others is first and foremost to improve colleagues' contribution to the quality of teaching and learning in the subject, as emphasized in the Secondary National Strategy materials.

Developing approaches to coaching that improve the quality of teaching and supporting colleagues (see Ritchie 2002, for an example of a whole-school approach) in making the most of assessment data are both challenges with significant relevance to personalizing learning and are, in some ways, subsets of a school's pedagogy. We have raised both processes (coaching and assessment) in earlier chapters. In this one, we are focusing on the subject leader's role. Subject leaders and other middle leaders responsible for teaching and learning can take on coaching roles and benefit from being coached by other more experienced leaders in developing their leadership capacity. In terms of being a coach, the subject leader should be in a position to support other colleagues in improving the quality of teaching in the subject. Subject leaders coaching others, particularly working within the whole-school's approach to assessment (and assessment for learning) is another contribution of the middle leadership level to personalizing learning.

A further dimension of a school's pedagogy is an understanding of how specific subjects fit into the wider curriculum and how subjects can contribute to broadening and enriching the curriculum in order that it provides potential for greater personalization. In other words, subject leaders should be engaging in whole curriculum development – working with others and representing and promoting the distinctive features of particular subjects and disciplines in such whole curriculum discussions. There are a range of innovative approaches to the whole curriculum in primary and secondary schools (especially in Year 7) that are being promoted by the Qualifications and Curriculum Authority (QCA) (www.qca.org.uk). There is an argument that, in more integrated approaches to the curriculum, the subject leader's role becomes redundant. We do not agree, whatever approach a school adopts to the curriculum (and we are advocates of integrated approaches that are well planned and well implemented). We think attention needs to be given to the distinctive nature of subjects as well as the similarities between them. There are, for example, interesting parallels between subjects like history and science in terms of the enquiry approaches involved. However, the nature of data and evidence (for example reliability and validity) and the representation of those data in accounts of enquiries are distinctly different. We see subject leaders as those best placed to represent the interests of particular subjects in discourse about the nature of the curriculum and its implementation. Keeping updated with developments within and across subjects is challenging and responsibility needs to be shared across the staff – allocation of subject leadership is a way of doing that.

Embracing creativity, culture and citizenship is, we would contend, another responsibility for all subject leaders. One of us has written, with others, about how these dimensions can be used to enrich the design and technology curriculum (Howe et al. 2001). In that book, case studies illustrate the impact that approaches to broadening the design and technology curriculum on improving the engagement of learners for personalizing their learning. All three dimensions are relevant in almost all subjects. Creativity is by no means limited to so-called 'creative' subjects like art and design. We, and others (NACCCE/DfEE 1999), see creativity as appropriate in all subjects.

Many subject leaders, especially in primary schools, bemoan the lack of time they have to be effective in their roles. Evidence (Bell and Ritchie 1999) suggests many would like to be doing more with respect to their subject roles if only they had the time and resources. One claim on a subject leader's time is that related to monitoring and evaluation. Subject leaders have, in a variety of ways and degrees of success in many schools, been systematically monitoring the quality of teaching and learning. In the past, one test of their effectiveness in this respect has been the outcome of their interviews with Ofsted inspectors during school inspections. In the new context of self-evaluation forms (SEFs) and short inspections, such interviews are less common and the contribution of subject leaders to monitoring is less obvious but nonetheless still vital, hence the challenge to find more creative ways to monitor. Self-evaluation is an increasingly significant aspect of the inspection process. One of us has written about the changing nature of school self-evaluation in England and Wales (Ritchie 2007b). Local evidence, from work with headteachers and subject leaders, suggests that practice varies enormously in terms of the direct contribution subject leaders make to formal school self-evaluation (and the SEF). We consider self-evaluation to be of value way beyond school inspection – it is a process essential to school improvement. If schools are to move towards more personalizing of learning, as a part of school improvement, then self-evaluation needs to be embraced. Subject leaders have a significant contribution to make to effective school self-evaluation.

The role of subject leaders in working with others has already been mentioned. However, one of the challenges listed refers specifically to collaborative school-based research. We have been involved in supporting school-based and teacher-led research for many years (Ollerenshaw and Ritchie 1997, especially Chapter 8; Ritchie 2001, especially Chapter 9) and, in many cases, a subject leader has been the key driver of the research endeavour. We see school and classroom research as one of the ways in which a school builds its understanding of pedagogy and a process by which developments can be systematically and rigorously evaluated in a formative way. Pupils also have a contribution to make to school-based research. They can be much more than mere respondents and objects of research. In some schools, pupils are becoming co-researchers with teachers. In others, the pupils lead research into learning.

Collaborative research within a school is desirable and has considerable potential. However, schools are increasingly involved in networks of other schools (as discussed in Chapter 3) and we would argue the potential of cross-school collaboration has enormous benefits as the NCSL's network learning community initiative has shown (Jackson 2002b). We have seen excellent examples of research being initiated, carried out, evaluated and disseminated through school networks – some local, others over a broader geographical area and some based on international networks.

We will now look at aspects of subject leadership in practice to illustrate some of the issues raised in the discussion above.

Middle leaders as agents of change

Primary Case Study

The following case study illustrates the work of a science subject leader whose experience of teaching science in a way that was personalizing the experience for her class was used to influence teaching and learning in another subject (literacy). We see her engaging with a number of the gateways to personalizing learning identified by Hargreaves (2004) including: curriculum development; assessment for learning; learning how to learn; and ICT. In this case study, we see examples of her leadership skills such as strategic thinking, role modelling, developing good professional relationships and so on.

Becci Digby is science subject leader at Hotwells Primary School in Bristol. She is also responsible for assessment and, at the time of the interview, was acting deputy headteacher.

Hotwells is a primary school previously identified and featured by one of us (Ritchie 2004) as a school where distributed leadership was embedded. Previous data collected from Becci and her head, Jenny Taylor, illustrated the extent to which Becci felt empowered, within the collaborative culture in the school, to take responsibility for developments. Her current focus has considerable relevance to personalizing learning and addresses approaches to assessment for learning. Interestingly, Becci described developing approaches to assessment for learning in literacy (wearing her 'assessment leader' hat) that grew out of her work in science.

Personalizing learning is a challenge that the school is taking very seriously and Becci recently led staff development for the Key Stage 2 team on this topic. The school has already adopted approaches to building learning power and uses the Effective Lifelong Learning Inventory (ELLI). They have been focusing on collaborative group-work and attainment-raising in mathematics and in writing.

During the INSET, Becci facilitated discussions of a strategic nature concentrating on Hargreaves' 'curriculum' gateway (2004). The team looked at the whole-school curriculum map to find ways of promoting key dimensions, such as collaborative work. They sought, using a focus on core skills, to find ways to reduce the curriculum burden on staff and pupils to avoid inappropriate repetition and allow more time to be given to topics that allow more personalized approaches. They were keen to increase the relevance of the curriculum and make the most of links to learning beyond the classroom. The teachers were interested in giving children more ownership of a particular topic. Becci and others in the KS2 team were concerned that ELLI was being used effectively at Key Stage 1 but was not as well embedded at Key Stage 2. The school was seeking to further embed the use of learning language as part of a learning-centred approach. The team were identifying which learning dispositions were appropriate to particular topics – for example, building learning relationships into a topic on the Egyptians and critical curiosity through a science topic.

Case Study, *cont.*

Assessment for learning was another gateway to personalizing learning that Becci was prioritizing in her middle leadership roles. Her own classroom work on assessment for learning (especially peer and self-assessment) had been shared with others to foster a whole-school approach, initially within Key Stage 2.

She had developed the use of concept mapping as a tool for peer, teacher and self-assessment in science in the context of her Advanced Skills Teacher (AST) role, which had given her time to visit other schools and for reflection. She had decided to adapt such approaches to literacy. In her view, time needed to be given to elicit from learners 'what they need to know' rather than making assumptions about it. In science she had evidence of pupils increasingly understanding their own learning needs and setting their own targets. In her experience, concept maps enable a teacher to gain insights into learners' current understanding and use that for planning the next steps. It is a way of valuing pupils' voice within the planning process. With younger children, when she was teaching Year 3 the previous year, the pupils' voices were captured on Post-it notes and used to create displays. She had developed the use of large format portfolios with these pupils to capture the story of their learning. These portfolios included peer and self-assessment of, for example, key skills. 'Science partners' would construct a shared concept map that would go in the portfolio. These were referred back to near the end of a topic to look for progress and to inform self-assessment against key skills. The portfolios act as a record for group, pair and individual learning.

This approach was adopted by other teachers for science – illustrating the value of Becci as a role model and as someone who is able, in a leadership role, to facilitate the learning of others and have an impact on their practice.

At Hotwells, Becci says the pupils generally have good speaking and listening skills and teachers are good at facilitating discussion among children (they use 'Philosophy for Children' to enhance this) but pupils are less successful with writing.

Consequently, Becci was keen to translate her good practice in science, which was working well, to the area of literacy and especially writing, where concerns across the school have been identified through analysis of assessment data and teachers' opinions.

Using a similar format, Becci encouraged pupils in her Year 6 class to set their own targets after self-assessing their writing based on her initial individual targets for them (as 'writing' profiles), informed by what they had previously done. The profiles (for factual and non-factual writing) were used across KS2. However, Becci felt the pupil-generated targets were not being used as well by the pupils as they had been in science. She talked to the class about how this situation could be improved. One solution was to integrate the process into the books in which the work was being done – to paste the target sheets, self-assessment and peer assessment into their books alongside the work. Gradually pupils took increasing ownership of the process and the books became the narrative through which their learning was recorded. The pupils had, as a consequence of the common 'learning language' that permeates the school's approach, appropriate language to set specific personal targets. Becci felt their engagement in self-assessment

Case Study, *cont.*

and peer assessment did lead to improved progress being made. Peer assessment was based on tools Becci provided including, for example, continua on which a peer rated a piece of work. The model is sophisticated and, to the outsider, initially looks complex. However, the pupils have helped construct the approach and confidently engage with it. It is complemented by a simple reward system.

Similarly, through the tangible examples that Becci could provide for colleagues in team discussions and one-to-one conversations, they were also able to see the benefits and adopt similar approaches in their own classrooms. Having moved from Year 3 to Year 6 this year, Becci felt increasingly aware of the need for progressive development of approaches to learning generally and within specific subjects such as science and literacy. The literacy subject leader is in KS1 and Becci recognized the need to ensure her work on assessment in literacy in KS2 built on work in KS1.

Becci's initiative provides a good example of formative 'assessment for learning' aimed at personalizing the learning of pupils in her class and throughout the school.

We explored another of the gateways to personalizing learning: ICT. She considers ICT to be well embedded in the school. She gave particular examples of how items such as digital cameras have been used as tools for self-assessment. Children are encouraged to capture themselves at work (for example in a practical investigation) and use the image (perhaps presented through the interactive whiteboard), to reflect on and share the learning that was taking place with the individual, group or whole class. This was an approach particularly valuable for learners with preferences for more visual and auditory styles.

Becci went on to discuss the approach to teamwork that the school is now evolving. Subject leaders are working together in teams focused on school-wide issues – for example, boys' writing. The headteacher values such approaches and facilitates it through ensuring time is available for the teams to meet regularly. In Becci's KS2 team, she initially took responsibility for setting the agenda but as time went on, others took more ownership of the agenda and have been raising issues. The forum has become a context for the whole team learning about how to get better at what they do. It is through these meetings that the approaches that Becci had used in her classroom have been disseminated and used as the basis for a consistent approach across the key stage (and, where appropriate, beyond). When possible, such discussions are informed by peer observations of each other's practice. Less experienced teachers are encouraged to observe more experienced teachers as well as the other way round. When Becci observes colleagues, the focus of the observation is negotiated and usually involves a focus on an aspect of learning rather than teaching. Becci also monitors through looking at pupils' books. Her AST role has given Becci an experience of approaches in other schools that she can use to inform team discussions. As assessment leader, she is constructing a portfolio of approaches to assessment that contributes to the school's self-evaluation and provides evidence for Ofsted. The team are keen to ensure as much consistency of approach as is possible.

Case Study, *cont.*

In all aspects of her role as a middle leader, Becci considers herself to be extremely well supported by her headteacher. This happens informally and more formally through regular conversations and meetings. In some things, for example, the analysis of the school's assessment data, Jenny and Becci work collaboratively together on the same task. In others, Jenny supports Becci directly (for example, through observing her classroom practice and providing feedback) or indirectly (through organizational structures or advice and resourcing).

Jenny Taylor shares Becci's view of the importance of personalizing learning and of peer and self-assessment as part of that. She also values the benefits of ELLI and its junior version, 'JELLI', and the seven dimensions of learning power as the foundation for a whole-school approach to learning, which brings shared language and understanding. Everyone at Hotwells is committed to innovative learning – for example, all staff (teaching and non-teaching) mentor children who need support (each member of staff meets with their one or two mentees weekly to review progress). This means that all staff are familiar with and using a shared language of learning. The language is embedded in the reward system, for example, the wording used on certificates. Parents have also increasingly become familiar with this language. Foundation-stage teachers have been working with teachers in other schools to make the learning language accessible to the youngest children.

We explored other aspects of personalizing learning that have engaged subject leaders and other staff, including:

- Improved use of the school's assessment data, including that from optional SATs alongside other assessment practices discussed above, for target setting and 'tracking back' to monitor progress.

- Curriculum development across the school to enable more personalized learning that is meaningful to individuals (and builds on the challenges and opportunities provided by *Excellence and Enjoyment*).

- Timing curriculum activities to motivate learners, for example, improving pupils' motivation in science by moving a topic like electricity to earlier in the year.

- Curriculum enrichment enhanced through better use of lunchtimes. Support staff are now leading sports activities and strategic games/creative activities during the lunch break.

- Other enrichment activities, such as the introduction of French and a better use of school camps.

- Ensuring equality of access to ICT for all pupils, especially those without access at home, through making the ICT suite available outside lesson time.

- Valuing student voice and providing more active engagement for pupils – through, for example, school council work focused on eco-school developments.

- Ensuring interventions to improve pupils' progress are focused – for example,

Case Study, *cont.*

Jenny is herself supporting those pupils thought capable of achieving level 5 at mathematics.

- Focusing on collaborative group-work to foster young people's capacity for group and independent learning (a focus in the school for many years).

- Using 'Philosophy for Children' across the school to develop young people's capacity for reasoning; listening to others; accepting constructive criticism and engaging in high-quality dialogue. (Training for this was provided for staff by the Society for the Advancement of Philosophical Enquiry and Reflection in Education, SAPERE (www.sapere.net), in 2003 and is supported through a school-developed pack and whole-school scheme.)

Subject leadership continues to be valued as an important aspect of middle leadership and a key dimension of distributed leadership despite the school moving towards more integrated approaches to the curriculum. Subject leadership of a specific subject is sometimes shared (for example, between two teachers who have just completed their NQT years). Some part-time staff have subject leadership roles. Subject leadership is also supported through the establishment of teams, as discussed above, through which subject leaders can share experience. These have been in place since September 2006.

We explored the role of middle leaders in school self-evaluation. Core subject leaders, the Foundation-stage team leader, the values team leader, the SENCO and ICT subject leader have all been actively engaged in discussions related to the self-evaluation form (SEF) and worked with Jenny on particular sections.

Secondary Case Study

In some schools, the process of personalizing learning for students is dependent on them having the necessary literacy skills to access the curriculum and actively engaging in learning to learn. Hengrove Community Arts College in Bristol is one such school. It is an 11–18 urban comprehensive school with an intake that draws on one of the most deprived wards in the country. The school found itself requiring special measures after an Ofsted inspection in November 2003. One of the key issues requiring attention was literacy, which was seen as inhibiting students' progress in other areas. At that time, Hannah Enticott was an English teacher responsible for KS3 English. She sought and was given the opportunity to initiate a project aimed at improving literacy across all subject areas. Below is a description of her work on the 'Literacy Across the Curriculum' (LAC) project, based on an account she wrote for a middle leadership course. It illustrates how a relatively inexperienced teacher was empowered by her headteacher, in a school where distributed leadership was encouraged, to take a leading role in a major school improvement initiative to establish the context in which learning could become more personalized. It was planned as a long-term sustainable school improvement initiative with support from the senior leadership team that would impact on students' performance.

The Hengrove Literacy Across the Curriculum (LAC) project was set up by Hannah to:

- Raise the profile and importance of literacy skills among all staff, students and parents at Hengrove Community Arts College.

- Develop resources, teaching strategies and a college-wide framework that would encourage a sustainable system for delivering, assessing and monitoring the quality of literacy skills across all faculties within the college.

- Create a forum for discussion, analysis and decision making for staff to share ideas around delivering literacy skills in the form of a LAC working group, which has a representative from every faculty and department at the college.

- Deliver literacy-based activities within pastoral time. The tasks were designed to reinforce key skills required by subjects across the curriculum. They also allow students an opportunity to gain support and confidence in these skills through tasks facilitated by tutors with whom they have a non-academic relationship.

- Improve students' achievements across the curriculum.

The project was started in January 2004. In the first year the following strategies were developed, piloted and evaluated:

- The LAC working group was established under her leadership with representatives from all subjects and met regularly. LAC was a team initiative involving shared problem-solving and collective action that required good professional relationships and shared ownership of the initiative.

- Use of good practice from her own practice and other members of the working group to inform developments – the intention was to build on local strengths.

- Two INSET sessions for the whole staff, led by Hannah, to introduce and maintain the profile of LAC and to ensure all staff, new or existing, were knowledgeable about the strategies and expectations of the project.

- All staff were provided with corporate resources developed by the working group – both for use with students in the classroom and to help subject staff develop appropriate resources for their subject needs.

- Lesson plans were monitored to ensure inclusion of literacy objectives and high-quality literacy foci and activities.

These strategies were monitored and evaluated in line with the expectations of the college, Her Majesty's Inspectors (HMI) and the staff involved. The initial evaluation formed the base of the next step of this project – developing a pastoral literacy programme with a focus on improving oracy skills among all students.

During 2005–2006, key developments included:

- The LAC working group continued to meet in order to evaluate the impact and develop the next set of literacy resources.

- The third in a series of staff development sessions was delivered during INSET time at the beginning of the academic year.

- The third set of corporate resources focusing specifically on encouraging oracy and self-assessment were developed and provided.

- Lessons were observed to ensure that high standards were maintained.

- Work by the LAC working group members with Full Service Extended School (FSES) initiative to run lunchtime activities focused on literacy.

- Work with FSES to provide community literacy sessions.

Hannah identified a range of factors leading to the initiative's success:

- Unconditional support from the senior leadership team that led to the team feeling empowered, enthusiastic and committed to the project.

- Ownership of the initiative by the middle leaders involved, especially those on the working group, through clear understanding of the purpose of the changes being introduced.

- Growing understanding of those directly involved in the project of how it was proving to be an 'innovation in distributed leadership'.

- Establishment of structures, such as the working group, which met monthly and proved sustainable over time.

- Evidence of impact on students' learning was clear from the first phase and validated by external scrutiny (HMI).

- Staff were encouraged to focus on the core values they held related to their subjects.

- Progress from leading faculties (English, Humanities and PE) was shared to inform others making less progress.

- Allocation of key literacy skills to specific faculties informed by a thorough audit.

- Validation of progress from HMI (in context of inspections while in special measures) of the 'effective leadership provided by the literacy group'.

- Success in moving responsibility for literacy 'from the exclusive control of the English faculty to a central responsibility held by all.'

In summary Hannah considers that 'united action had created individual success'. The school came out of requiring special measures in 2006 and the literacy initiative was clearly part of the reason for the transformation of the school. The LAC has, in her view, become embedded in the practice of Hengrove. The work is ongoing and the focus for the future is further attention to Key Stage 4.

Both of these case studies provide examples of middle leaders as agents of change. The teachers involved were developing leadership skills and capacity – learning to be effective leaders – as they implemented changes aimed at improving the opportunities for young people.

Conclusion

This chapter has highlighted the contribution to personalizing learning for students of middle leaders. Middle leaders, unlike most headteachers, are in a unique position of being change agents in their own classrooms and across the school. This enables them to offer colleagues role models as teachers, which is more difficult for headteachers to do. Middle leaders are absolutely grounded in the reality of real classrooms and are therefore more likely to understand the challenges that other teachers will face in implementing proposed changes. The role of middle leaders as agents of change is also made more challenging because they are both teachers and leaders. Indeed, they are sometimes simultaneously learners, teachers and leaders. While Ofsted and others have emphasized the significance of headteachers to successful schools, Ofsted have over many years also acknowledged the contribution of effective subject leaders to successful schools. In our experience, any school that successfully implements more personalized approaches to learning will have drawn on the leadership capacity of middle leaders. They are a group who perhaps most obviously gain from the opportunities distributed leadership offers. We have seen examples in both the case studies of distributed leadership in action. These are not stories of heads merely delegating responsibilities to others, they are examples of strong heads who recognize that, by empowering middle leaders, they can increase the leadership capacity of their schools and pupils can benefit from the improvements that can be envisioned, planned and implemented by such colleagues.

Chapter 7

The role of teachers and pupils as leaders: learning and leading – a participatory pedagogy

Introduction

In this chapter we will explore how learning and leadership are deeply interconnected at the level of the learning and teaching encounter. We have seen how personalizing learning means attending to the unique 'self' of the learner in their encounter with the knowledge, skills and understanding which are part of the 'publicly required' curriculum. This includes their particular story and their natural and personal power to learn. When learning is understood as a journey, then it follows that each unique learner may follow a particular pathway and have an individual destination in mind. It is here that leadership and power become very significant because the goal of personalizing learning, and a crucial goal for democracy, is that our schools produce individuals who are *able to take responsibility for their own learning journey and to do so in a way that respects other people's learning and contributes to a sustainable social world.*

The implication of this is that teaching is about progressively letting go of power and empowering learners to take responsibility for leading themselves. This, of course, requires considerable expertise and courage on the part of teachers. Supporting learners in taking responsibility for themselves means being neither highly controlling nor *laissez-faire*. Rather it means finding an appropriate balance between structure and nurture, between rigour and creativity, between the personal and the public – holding the two in creative tension. For this, teachers themselves need to be able to take responsibility for their own professional judgements and their own professional learning in the classroom, and thus create and model the sort of climate and relationship that are conducive for personalized learning and distributed leadership.

Taking responsibility for my own learning journey

Being competent to manage the tension between innovation and continuity, a core competence we have discussed in Chapter 4, requires a person to be able to become aware of, and take responsibility for, their own intentions, actions and choices and to be able to discriminate between different good things, over time. It requires a sense of moral responsibility since human actions have an impact on other people. At the heart of this is the idea of agency; that is, the capacity of a person to take responsibility for himself in relation to others and to the environment, constructing an identity which is not unthinkingly defined by current social values, patterns and interpretations.

Learning how to learn is more than simply managing the skills and strategies necessary to achieve a particular goal. It is about becoming an agent of one's own learning and changing, and for teachers as leaders this dimension of changing and learning applies to the whole community. To do this a person needs to become aware of and understand his own identity as a learner, and over time, take responsibility for his own learning journey. This requires the learner to have a vision of where he wants to be – in one week, or one year or ten years – and to progressively take responsibility for the steps needed to achieve that vision. This means securing the support of others in that vision and staying motivated in moving towards it. Teachers are leaders in this long and complex journey – they have a vision of their students as effective lifelong learners and they bring about change for improvement in the service of that vision. They are required to relate that vision both to learners as unique individuals and to their learners as a group – and this is a constant tension in the journey if personalization is a goal.

For teachers this requires a shift from viewing teaching as the process of providing information, and learning as the process of receiving it, to a shared process between learner and teacher. Learning which is personalized is learning in which leadership is progressively handed over to the learner. This means teachers are sharing power and control with students, which is an act of distributed leadership. McCombs and Miller (2006: 9) say to teachers that: 'Sharing power and control with your students and viewing yourself as a learner assists your students in understanding that when learners of any age feel ownership of their learning, by virtue of having a voice and choice, they are more willing to learn and be involved in their learning.'

It is in this sense that a person's learning journey requires distributed leadership, which is an 'emergent property of a group or network of individuals in which group members pool their expertise' (Gronn 2002a). Most learners, including the most advanced adult learners, need to interact with other people in their learning. Distributing the responsibility for learning, like distributing leadership, creates an amount of learning power that is greater than the sum of the individual parts. Distributed leadership operates in and through relationships, and is shared between learners and teachers – so much so that teachers are really learning guides. They are more advanced learners who mentor and coach less experienced learners in their own unique learning journeys. This ether of relationships is crucial to learning and leadership, and yet it is often the most difficult element to define and quantify with hard evidence.

Choice and voice: the learning self

There is an important relationship between the development of self-regulating learners and learning that is personally relevant and meaningful. Meaning making is one of the seven dimensions of learning power, and it is important because it is through meaning making that learning connects with the self and the stories of the learner. When what is being learned has some personal, real-life meaning for the learner then he or she is more likely to be willing to take responsibility for his or her learning. Students are motivated by the opportunity for personal choice and meaning making, and this particularly applies to disaffected and disengaged learners.

Our choices are direct reflections of who we are as human beings. The less choice a person has, the more important very small choices become, because choice enables us to express our identity and says something about who we are, and what matters to us. Being given the opportunity to express choices and preferences through respectful listening and speaking is more than something necessary for survival in global democracies – it is fundamentally about valuing the person and the stories and cultures that have shaped that person's identity.

In one of our research and development projects in the West Country, the responsibility for choosing a starting point for a personalized learning project was given directly to the students. The key ideas were introduced in Chapter 2. These students were mostly 17 year olds and included some very able Year 11 students, a group of learners 'not in education employment and training' and a group in a secure unit for young offenders. None of these young people were used to having choice in their learning – since almost always their starting point for learning, and their ending points, have been given by the public requirements of the curriculum and its assessment framework. They had to learn to choose before they could begin. They had to identify 'what it feels like to be interested in something' and how to bring their own interests and stories into the classroom.

When these students settled on a concrete object, artefact or experience that was personally meaningful to them, as a starting point for a personalized project, then their learning was significantly enhanced because they had a personal investment in it. It was more than simply the acquisition of other people's knowledge – it was *personal*. Their power to learn was scaffolded through using the seven dimensions of learning power to support progressively higher-order types of thinking and learning. The final product was assessed in a manner negotiated with the learners themselves.

What was significant in this project was that its crucial value was in putting the person at the centre of learning. One of the learners, Jonathan, who participated in the research, put it this way: 'It all ties together – it's about self-awareness more than anything else...to choose your objects you need to understand yourself and your own story and you have to be self-aware...self-awareness is not even touched upon in the education system...part of the self-awareness thing is to tell your own story' (Deakin Crick et al. 2007b: 17).

And another student, Melza, added: 'Learning how to tell your own story would make it easier to do all the other things you have to do – learn subjects, get grades etc.' (Deakin Crick et al. 2007b: 17).

Leading or following

Melza and Jonathan went on to compare their experience in this research project to their experiences within a National Curriculum framework working for public examinations, in which they felt that what and how they learned were already prescribed for them. They were not given the power to lead in their own learning. They had to follow the same pathway as everyone else, which Melza thought was 'a trust thing'. She went on to say 'we are all programmed in a way that makes our experience invisible'.

Yet it is when the learner's personal experience connects with their learning that they are empowered and able to negotiate their own pathways. Another student in this project was quite damning about syllabus-driven learning in mainstream classrooms: 'Doing this project has allowed me to remove myself from the monotony of my usual courses and how they are taught, it gave me an opportunity to almost teach myself and to realise for myself the incorrect way of doing things, instead of just being told what's wrong...As an alternative to learning how the syllabus dictates I have discovered how to learn as an individual; rather than as the rest of the students in the room are being taught. In a classroom every student is taught as though they were the same person, outside of it you can choose which ways your mind will best process the task at hand' (Deakin Crick et al. 2007b: 18).

This impatience with a 'one size fits all' experience of secondary education was echoed by Richard from the Education to Employment course, speaking for his peer group: 'Students often don't get on with school because every student has to do the same work, you all do one thing. They need more choice in approach – it gives you more freedom to decide instead of depending on what the teacher wants' (Deakin Crick et al. 2007b: 18).

Teacher professional learning and choice: the learning self

Personalized learning not only requires teachers to distribute leadership but also to take responsibility for their own professional choices. In a system and curriculum in which the outcomes are predefined, the curriculum is prescribed and the pedagogy is preset, there is little room for professional discernment on the part of teachers. Yet if each learner is unique and walks on a particular, personalized pathway, there can be no preset formula for success, although there will be signposts and indicators along the way.

Thus the task of professional leadership for the teacher in the classroom is really important – she must be sufficiently confident of her vision, and the principles and practices that will lead her students towards that vision. By holding this in mind she can diagnose, intervene and provide guidance in multiple unique learning situations throughout the week. By reflecting on and learning about concrete classroom experiences and interactions, she mindfully offers leadership in learning to her students, *and shares the responsibility for leadership in learning with them.*

Thus she has choice and ownership of her personally owned pedagogy and is able to model and offer leadership, and draw on her own experience as a professional. The metaphor of the jazz player helps us to understand this. The jazz player plays with a team, and together they understand, as they have experienced the rules and principles of jazz – the particular combinations of chords and melodies and the iterations and responses to each musical contribution, sometimes together and sometimes solo. However they do not play other people's written music – rather they improvise and create something new each time. It is still recognizably jazz but it creates the spaces for wonderful moments and experiences that are unique and often unrepeatable. In the same way, the teacher draws on her experiences and the principles of learning to improvise and create a climate where 'magic moments' of learning occur. These moments are incredibly hard to measure or evaluate, but we have never met a teacher who does not know what they are nor recognize them when they occur.

Learning pathways: top-down or bottom-up?

One of the real challenges today is how to create curricula where students are able to choose, and follow uniquely chosen and personally meaningful pathways through the content of the curriculum *and at the same time* acquire the skills, knowledge and understanding that are their entitlement, and achieve the rigour and discipline of a particular subject or domain which is examined publicly.

The idea of learning pathways was introduced in Chapter 2, in which we described eight steps identified from research projects that are like stepping stones to personalized learning. We later talked about the stations of the learning journey, beginning with the learning self, moving through the personal power to learn, to publicly valued competencies and finally publicly valued learning outcomes. Making the connection between personally constructed knowledge and the resources and know-how that is enshrined in the scholarship of the public world is a key part of the journey. Jess, on the Education to Employment project, began with her personal place of interest, which was Cheddar Gorge. As she began to describe the gorge, and the reasons she was so profoundly personally interested in it, she identified a key theme in her learning – what happened before? It was at this point she realized that there is a wealth of historical resources out there that she could connect to, and her final assessment was a leaflet that reflected a journey through time, from cave men to her present-day experience.

Jess was enthusiastic in her final debrief after her project: 'It's made me not so scared to learn other things,' she said. 'It was a tiny little project and it spiralled into all these other things that were connected.' For her it was a key time of attitude change. 'I didn't think I could learn anymore, but now I believe I can.' She was able to reflect on 'how deep [her project] went, it's not just about Cheddar Gorge, it's about life stuff' (Deakin Crick et al. 2007b: 16).

This methodology has also been used successfully at degree level, where it is described as a process that links the academic and contextual, the universal and the local, the objective with the subjective and the personal with the public (Jaros and Deakin Crick, 2006).

Teachers' learning pathways

One of the characteristics of education as a discipline is that it is inescapably about the interaction of theory with practice and practice with theory. Like medicine, it is *practised* and its overarching purpose is for the well-being of the community. A huge challenge in education is to find ways of working, both structures and processes, in which research, practice and policy are integrated: in other words to create professional learning communities where there are shared languages and academic research is demystified for teachers while at the same time real-life classroom experience is reflected in research in a participatory pedagogy. When teachers reflect on concrete classroom experiences, begin to ask questions and problematize particular practices, and search for explanations and solutions, then they are both learning *and* exercising distributed leadership. They are contributing to the learning of the community. When these questions lead them to make meaningful connections with the scholarship of the wider educational community, then the potential for extending leadership is exponential.

Teachers as leaders of learning: learning relationships

The skill of the teacher in leading learners through their particular learning pathways is crucial. A participatory pedagogy, such as this, is a 'relational' one – that is, one that focuses on the needs and character of the 'learner-in-community' as a context for approaching individual and broader social needs. The teacher is better described as a learning guide and the relationship between the learner and the learning guide frames and infuses all pedagogical activities.

In *Learning by Accident*, a report of one of the personalized learning projects with disengaged learners described above, Milner (2006) identified the following key values for creating 'spaces of trust' where learners can practise 'taking responsibility for their own learning':

- The teacher is a '**learning guide**' who:

    a) is committed to the development of his or her learners and
    b) has some prior knowledge of the pathways and subject matter but *not* that he or she possesses knowledge which the other must acquire.

- Learners are treated and referred to in the manner of '**co-researchers**', that is, with equal status to the learning guide. Their input (positive and negative) is recognized as invaluable to the further development of the scheme.

- '**Conversations**' between learner and learning guide form the cornerstone of the developing process. Here, learners can freely articulate concerns, doubts and positive feedback, without the judgements of the whole class.

- The learning guide's first priority is to the young person's forming **life narrative**, rather than to learning objectives.

- The priority is to **listening**, over instructing, in these conversations: the guide should aim to *enable* the individual's telling of their own story (in the manner of a psychotherapist at times – searching intuitively for 'clues' from which to make suggestions) rather than to direct it.

- **Rationale, limits and expectations** must be made clear and adhered to: the progressions need to be structured in such a way that the learner feels secure, and does not fear imminent exposure or failure.

- **Encouragement** should accompany and precede all suggestions, target setting and assessment activities.

- The space created must be one where an individual may speak freely; this requires a commitment to **open-mindedness and non-judgement**, especially if young people test the relationship by attempting to shock.

- **Evaluation** gives the process a value – individual and group sessions critiquing the process and reflecting on progress play a vital role in facilitating ownership.

- The **optional** nature of the project must be emphasized (especially in a secure setting) and the learner's choice to withdraw must be respected even if reasons seem irrational.

Positive interpersonal relationships are equally crucial to distributed leadership as to learning. We discussed reciprocal interdependency in Chapter 3 where one leader's practice becomes the basis for another leader's practice, and the circulation of initiative where an individual initiates change and this contributes to the flow of learning in the organization. Crucially, the characteristics of relationships for learning and for leadership are trust, respect and challenge. These materialize through modelling, monitoring and dialogue.

Building the personal power to learn: scaffolding the journey

The process of the learning guide gradually handing over responsibility for learning to the learner takes place through 'scaffolding'. This involves monitoring, formative and dynamic assessment and dialogue that is designed to enable the learner to progressively take responsibility for themselves. The purpose of scaffolding is to provide a secure framework for a wall or a building while it is in the process of being constructed or repaired. Once it is secure enough to stand on its own foundation then the scaffolding is removed. Learner-centred teachers scaffold learning in the same sense – the whole purpose of the exercise is for the learner to 'stand in their own foundations'. Whether the learner is a student or a teacher, similar principles apply. The teacher is a guide, a coach or a mentor.

The seven dimensions of learning power offer a form of scaffolding that enables the learner to reflect on themselves and their learning identity and motivation, and forwards towards the learning outcome, or achievement goal. For example, when the learners in the project described above were asked to make a choice about their starting point, their teacher scaffolded their choice by introducing the learning power dimensions. Feedback from each learner's profile enabled them to reflect on themselves as learners, their likes and dislikes, strengths and areas for development. They then focused on 'creativity' – embodied in the cartoon character of Bart Simpson – and 'idea spinning' in which they selected as many possible options as they could. Next they invoked 'strategic awareness' – this time embodied in Marge from *The Simpsons* – and reflected on their feelings of being interested and motivated to find out more.

Scaffolding operates at every stage of the learning journey – for example, invoking someone's critical curiosity and learning how to ask interesting questions of data is a key part of all self-regulated learning. Making connections between what is already known and new learning is another form of higher-order thinking which moves learners beyond the repetition of knowledge, through comprehension, application, analysis, synthesis and evaluation (Bloom 1956).

Competencies for leading and learning

Learning how to learn and distributing leadership are core competencies necessary for survival. They involve more than simply the accumulation of knowledge, but also personal values and attitudes, strategies, routines and management capacity. They are acquired through practice and commitment – we may say that the only difference between leading one's own learning and distributed leadership in the classroom is that of the level of responsibility – the former responsibility is to the self, while the latter is to the community. Both competencies are mutually dependent and foundational for active citizenship and life in the information age.

Leadership for learner-centred practices: creating a culture for learning

Research into learner-centred practices suggests that learning is non-linear, recursive, continuous, complex, relational and natural for human beings. It also suggests that learning happens best where learners have supported relationships, a sense of ownership and control over the learning process, and have safe and trusting learning relationships. McCombs (2006: 25) identifies the key processes involved in developing learner-centred principles and practices in classrooms and schools:

- Building ways to meet learner needs for interpersonal relationships and connections.
- Finding strategies that acknowledge individual differences and the diversity of learner needs, abilities and interests.
- Tailoring strategies to differing learner needs for personal control and choice.
- Assessing the efficacy of instructional practices to meet diverse and emerging individual learner and learning community needs.

She goes on to argue that it is not only important to match principles with practices, but to assess the match or mismatch with individual learners and their diverse needs. In other words, there is no single formula for becoming learner centred. Rather the teacher, as a learning guide, takes responsibility for leading the process of learning in ways that are reflexive and responsive to that particular community and its individual learners. The learning community and school is a complex living system. The learner-centred framework she describes reminds us that the human element cannot be left out of even the most technically advanced educational system.

One of the key features of teachers who are learner centred, according to McCombs' research, is that they are highly supportive of student autonomy and are not highly controlling. In a study one of us completed with nearly 900 students between the ages of 9 and 15, plus their teachers, we found that teachers who reported themselves to be highly controlling in their classrooms tended to have students in their classes who reported *low* levels of learning power, who did *not* find their school to be an emotionally safe place, and whose average achievement, by National Curriculum outcomes was lower (Deakin Crick et al. 2007). This points towards an ecology for learning characterized by distributed leadership, positive interpersonal relationships, respect and self-regulated learning.

As we have seen distributed leadership refers as well to the conditions in which people exercise leadership and the inter-relationships through which it operates. A learning-centred leadership creates a climate conducive to learning, and a learner-centred teacher powerfully creates such a climate within the classroom *and* contributes to that climate within the school. Indeed a teacher's learning through the experience of leading in the classroom inevitably generates leadership capacity across the school, and across the system as we shall see in the following case study from one primary school.

Learning engineers:
Jo's story of leadership and learning

Jo Stephens is a Year 5 teacher in Christchurch Primary School in Bristol. She was a lead teacher in a project working with five other local schools in partnership with the University of Bristol. The project was designed so that the schools could work collaboratively to enable children to develop a love of learning and the dispositions, values and attitudes necessary for effective lifelong learning. The focus was on the development of a shared language for learning and the creation of a climate for effective learning. Along with Year 5 teachers from the other schools, Jo developed a curriculum resource based on Isambard Kingdom Brunel – the famous Bristol engineer, whose work was being celebrated across the city 200 years after he died. The idea was to use the seven dimensions of learning power to scaffold a learning journey through the story of Brunel and his engineering achievements. The resource, called Brunelli, offered 'ready to go' learning opportunities to inspire teachers, which were rooted in real-life experience for the student, and which made the links with the seven dimensions of learning power explicit in the process and content of suggested lesson plans. An example of a sample lesson plan for science and design technology can be seen in Figure 7.

This represented considerable 'circulation of initiative' and shared professional learning. In particular we can see the development of an iconography of learning, where the seven dimensions of learning power are represented for teachers and students by simple icons which carry meaning and remind learners how they can progress through the subject matter. As researchers we had not seen this before. It is an example of leadership and learning from Jo, in collaboration with her colleagues – producing practices so seemingly powerful that they invite further research and move the professional learning agenda forwards. For example, when you come across this symbol you know you have to think of how what you are learning connects with what you already know, or have experienced.

Jo contributed to a whole-school INSET day, in which she modelled the practices she had developed in her classroom to other teachers; the whole school, especially the headteacher, shared the values of becoming learner centred and developing a language of learning. Each week, an assembly introduced one of the dimensions of learning power through the seven animals that the schools had chosen to represent them.

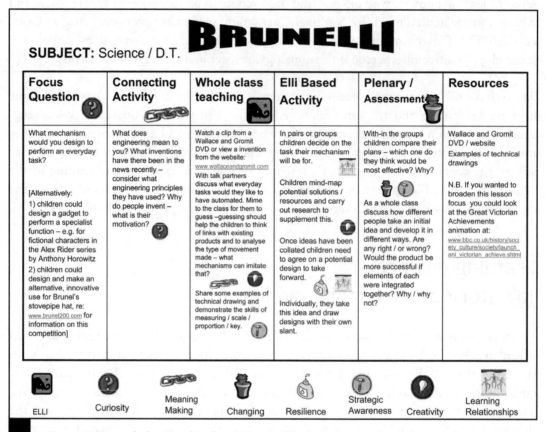

Figure 7: Example lesson plan for design technology

Jo gave her class the opportunity to produce straplines which summarized what the dimensions meant to them as learners and which were displayed in the classroom:

Creativity sparks your imagination and helps you throughout the day

Figure 8: Creativity strapline and unicorn metaphor

She led class discussions on learning power, developed classroom displays and specifically focused on student self-evaluation of their own learning journey. She created a 'Post-it' wall where students could post their 'wonder questions' and review their skills, involving parents and carers in the process. She invited her students to reflect on themselves as learners, and to develop their own identities, owning their personal power to learn. The drawings below show Jo's description of herself as a learner through identification with the learning power qualities of the particular animals that the students adopted to carry the message. She was modelling learning self-awareness for her students using their images!

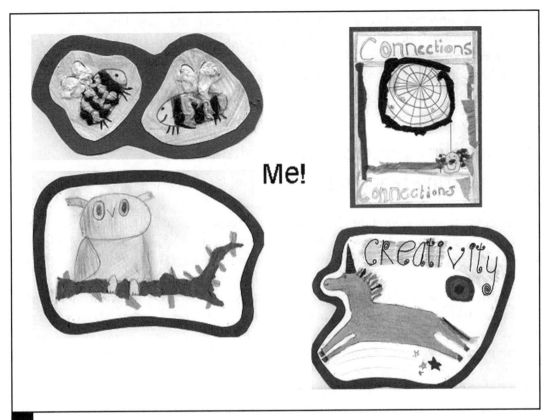

Figure 9: Simple self-assessment designed to stimulate self-awareness, ownership and responsibility for learning

The whole focus for her learners was for them to begin to understand themselves as learners and to take responsibility for their own learning; to identify for themselves ways forwards that recognized their strengths and individuality. When they evaluated how they were doing, some of the young learners said:

- 'I think I've got better at awareness because I am better at telling if I am doing well enough on my work.'

- 'I think I've been very creative at designing uses for Brunel's hat.'

- 'I think I've got a lot better at changing because I have put a lot of effort into improving my work.'

- 'I think I've got a lot better at curiosity because I always ask questions when I don't understand things.' (Small and Burn 2006)

Jo was exercising leadership in several ways:

- in relation to her own professional learning

- in relation to the school's shared vision for learning

- in relation to sharing leadership with her students so that they could learn for themselves

- in relation to the educational community by developing successful new ideas and practices which can move our thinking forwards.

She made connections between this work and other key priorities in her school – social, emotional and affective learning, *Every Child Matters* and *Healthy Schools* and *Investors in People*. She found being part of a network of teachers beyond her own school, including the university, a powerful stimulant for confidence in her own professional leadership.

Personalizing professional development – personalizing teaching

Jo's story offers some insight into how professional development can also be personalized. Here was a project that was personally meaningful to her and consistent with her own vision for learning and education. She identified with the task and brought her considerable creative resources to bear in applying the ideas of learning power to her classroom, in a unique and bespoke kind of way, for example, in the straplines that appeared in her classroom and in her presentations to other teachers about her work. In many ways she was modelling in her project the sorts of qualities and skills that she was hoping to encourage in her learners. She was able to draw upon the resources of colleagues in other schools and on a research base of knowledge in the local university. In this way, her own learning story connected with the shared local story of the Brunelli project across several schools and with the 'system-wide' story of education policy, with its focus on assessment for learning and creativity and enjoyment. Such personalization of teaching is likely to keep her vision for teaching alive, rather than see her resilience for learning drop off as her career develops (Day and Saunders 2006).

Conclusion

In this chapter we have explored how distributed leadership and personalizing learning are potent partners in the learning and teaching encounter in the classroom. We have seen how the goal of personalized learning is for each unique individual to become aware of and take responsibility for their own learning journey, leading themselves towards their personally chosen goal. The classroom teacher too, is a leading learner, but he or she has the additional responsibility, as a more advanced learner who knows something about the terrain, to support the learning journeys of her students, and to contribute to the shared organizational learning of the school.

Chapter Eight

Leadership development for personalized learning

Introduction

In this final chapter we draw together the themes of the book, in order to distil some of the key elements of a model for leadership development. In Chapter 1 we described the movement from an educational system that was shaped in the industrial era to one that is appropriate for the information age; from a mechanical metaphor of knowledge production to an ecological metaphor of sustainable learning. This sort of paradigm shift presents deep challenges to models of leadership: the new educational imaginary requires the distribution of power within a living system, in which individuals and the system itself are capable of continual and reciprocal learning and renewal.

Hargreaves (2004) suggests that personalizing means taking a novel angle on current practice and innovation. Working with school leaders, he identified nine gateways that are applicable to all schools and classrooms. These require strong and distributed leadership which enhances student motivation and learning. We have suggested that these are gateways to deep pedagogy rather than pedagogy that simply follows preset formulae, or strategies, and focuses mainly on measurable outcomes. Deep pedagogy means deep learning, both by students and their teachers; it means deep experience for learners, which is context based and meaningful to their stories and experience – through personalized curriculum supported by new technologies; it means deep support, through high quality interpersonal relationships expressed in mentoring and coaching, workforce development and personalized teaching; and it means deep leadership, which is learning centred, distributed through people and structures and embedded in school organization and design.

Throughout the book, we have explored the interconnections between distributed leadership and personalizing learning as they apply to these practical gateways and to the different roles and relationships of people in schools. We have used the metaphor of a learning journey, with stations that are attended to along the way: the learning self; the personal power to learn; publicly valued competencies and learning outcomes. The journey is relational and ecological – both leadership and learning are key variables in a living, learning system that adapts and changes in complex and sometimes unpredictable ways. The personal is as important as the public, and the journey is as important as the destination.

Creating a learning place

The challenge for leaders is to create the optimum conditions for learning, change and growth in individuals, the organization and the community. The creation of such a learning place has a distinctive presence, or atmosphere. Williams (2007: 224) defines this notion of a place as: 'The self-sustaining deep structure which is created when a number of people with shared intention successfully commit to mutually supporting each other in achieving their intention over an extended period of time.'

Williams' grounded theory research explores the nature of a therapeutic community, in which she finds that deep learning is taking place as well as therapeutic growth. This concept of place is equally applicable to a learning community – in which personal development and growth are also characteristic processes. Creating this place for learning requires particular personal, technical and organizational competencies on the part of its leaders. It allows for a more integral vision of education – one in which the exhausted language and values of rigid oppositions, and the linear rationality of cause and effect are replaced by an integral language, and the more holistic concept of emergence through relational connectivity.

Holland (1998) characterizes 'emergence' as change that occurs through interconnected networks, in which the whole is more than the sum of the parts and context determines function. New phenomena are persistent patterns with changing components, leading to new generic trends. Innovation and leadership have to do with identifying the key components for learning and constructing new and coherent combinations of these components.

We have suggested, in Chapter 5, that the challenge for leadership is to be able to hold in creative tension elements that may seem mutually incompatible, so that innovation, learning and growth can emerge. We have identified several familiar tensions throughout this book that represent a particular challenge for school leaders and policy makers – for example, the tension between freedom and limits, between autonomy and control and between the personal and the public perspectives.

Schools as living systems

Attending to all three human interests, in a dynamic learning journey, is best understood through an ecological metaphor – the school as a living system, rather than as a machine. In systems thinking, nothing exists independent of its relationship with others and what is critical is the relationship that is created between two or more elements. As Wheatley (1999: 36) puts it, 'Systems influence individuals and individuals call forth systems. It is the relationship that invokes the present reality. Which potential becomes real depends on the people, the events and the moment.'

She goes on to suggest that organizational power is purely relational. It is the capacity generated by relationships. Because power is energy, it needs to flow through organizations and what gives its charge, positive or negative, is the nature of relationships. When power is shared, as in distributed leadership and personalized learning, creative power abounds, and this has a positive impact on outcomes and personal satisfaction.

The conditions and context of learning created by the distribution of leadership support individual learners' needs, capacities, experiences and interests: that is, they support personalization. McCombs (2006) draws our attention to the personal domain of education, which is concerned with the human processes that operate on and/or are supported by the standards, curriculum, instruction and assessment components in the technical domain. The personal domain is also fundamental to the organizational domain that is concerned with the management structure, decision-making processes and policies that support the people and content requirements of education. That is, the personal domain emphasizes personal and interpersonal relationships, beliefs and perceptions that are affected by and/or supported by the organization and educational system as a whole.

In many schools, self-evaluation efforts focus primarily on technical issues (for example, high academic standards, increased student attainment, alignment of curricula and assessment, value for money) that serve and emphasize accountability. High-stakes testing places the brunt of accountability for student attainment on teachers, carrying punitive consequences for them as well as for students when standards are not met. To bring the system into balance the focus must also be on personal issues and the needs of all people in the system, including students and the adults who serve them in the teaching and learning process (McCombs & Miller 2006).

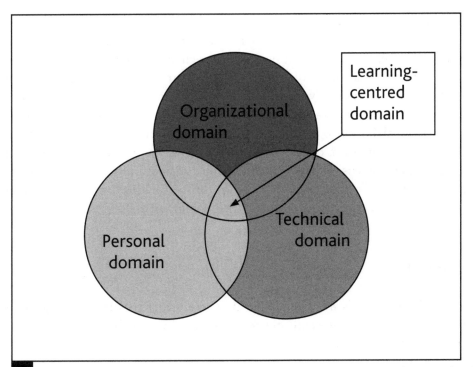

Figure 10: Balancing three domains for distributed leadership and personalized learning

Self-sustaining learning communities: self-evaluation as a modus operandi for leadership

Set formulas for managing change no longer exist (if they ever did) and the shift from accountability through inspection to accountability through self-evaluation is one of the characteristics of the changing paradigm that is crucially important for leadership. At the heart of self-evaluation is the process of knowledge co-creation and professional and organizational learning: that is, the collaborative capacity to identify questions, gather relevant data, assimilate and evaluate it and to use the new knowledge to devise solutions that move the learning community forwards in meeting its vision.

In Chapter 4 we argued that personalized learning and distributed leadership require schools to be characterized by technical, hermeneutical and emancipatory interests: that is by strategic and technical competence, by communicative and interpretive social practices and by personal and social practices that encourage all participants and the community as a whole to achieve their full potential and well-being. This requires leaders who are proficient in all three modes: they have technical skills and competencies, they have interpersonal skills and competencies and they are able to integrate their personal inner life and aspirations with their professional outer life and vision.

This is an integral vision for leadership that does not follow a set formula but rather holds together tensions in a creative and dynamic journey. A creative tension exists when there is a gap between two apparent opposites – such as continuity and innovation. The gap between the two is a source of energy since there are pulls in both directions within a learning community. A creative tension requires resolution or release – and the skill of leadership is in holding on to a vision and integrating the two polarities into something new, rather than giving in to either one. The tension is creative when a leader is able to integrate the preservation of tradition where that is important with innovation and change. Managing the tension between innovation and continuity is a 'meta competence' (Haste 2001), which is crucial for leadership for personalized learning. School self-evaluation is its modus operandi in the learning community.

Core values

An ecological metaphor is not value neutral. There are factors that we suggest inhibit learning and growth and some core spiritual and moral values that are foundational and vision forming for leadership.

Some of the core values underpinning this vision are described in the following table – although different groups may use a different language, we believe that there is an important underlying set of principles or core moral and spiritual values around empowerment, human value and social justice which shape this vision.

Core values	What do these look like?
Participation (versus exclusion)	Shared co-constructed values and vision as opposed to imposed institutional values and vision. Power is shared appropriately.
Trust (versus fear)	High levels of interpersonal trust as opposed to a culture of fear. Risk taking, creativity and individuality are valued and supported.
Changing and learning (versus being static)	Student and teacher identities are fluid. There is a shared belief that everyone can change and grow. Intelligence is multifaceted, and assessment practices support the processes of learning. There is an openness to change.
Human value (versus technical value)	Each person is valued: emotions are valued and managed, not ignored. Individuals are empowered to take responsibility for themselves and their own learning and growth.
Relationships (versus competitive individualism)	Relationships are important and are attended to. A culture of collaboration as opposed to a culture of individualism prevails. Reciprocal interdependence rather than dependence. Schools are part of wider networks.
Engaged, meaningful curricula (versus imposed curricula)	The curriculum is flexible, and relevant. It combines 'top down' rigour, with 'bottom-up' personalization.

Figure 11: Core values for leadership

In the next section, we explore some creative tensions in more detail; first considering the learning self: student, teacher and headteacher, secondly the learning organization and thirdly the school system.

Creative tensions: the learning self

For all learners, a creative tension that has appeared throughout the book is that between *continuity* and *change*. A sense of identity depends to some degree on stability and continuity but the capacity to be responsive, creative and open to change is crucial for all new learning. Making sense of one's own learning journey and integrating earlier experiences with new ones is crucial to meaning making – itself a key dimension of learning power. This is facilitated through narrative. Telling my story *and* having my story being heard, is a way of integrating this tension and allowing new learning to emerge.

Another key tension for the learning self is that between 'deeply personal' and 'publicly valued' learning outcomes. Focusing only on one or the other is inadequate and negotiating between personally meaningful choice and the rigour of the publicly valued examination, or qualification, is an important tension for teachers and students alike. How to engage all learners, and then scaffold the journey between the personal and the public remains a key challenge for assessment as well as for the sequencing of the curriculum. Once we take this tension into account seriously, then we come to value difference and diversity in communities and traditions and integrate personal development with achievement – we have an integral curriculum.

We have argued throughout the book that relationships of all sorts form the ether of distributed leadership and learning power. Being truly interdependent means sometimes being able to work independently and sometimes being able to work with others. This is a creative tension – but if a learner is isolated, or dependent on others, then it is not creative; rather it is a negative energy in the system.

For teachers there is a tension between being a good technician – having the strategies and deploying the skills of the technical domain – and being a creative professional. Holding this tension in balance is a question of purpose. In our view technical skills serve the purpose of creative professionalism, rather than being an end in themselves. In the end, a teacher's professional discernment, especially when honed by years of experience, is the most valid means of assessment of a learning outcome because it can incorporate technical, communicative and emancipatory interests in the context of a relationship and community.

For leaders, there is a creative tension between being a leader who lets go and being a follower. To truly distribute leadership, those in formal, designated authority are required to be open to learning from, and being led by, the least experienced on occasions. This demands professional humility and a relational ethic, rather than an individualistic, competitive ethic.

Creative tensions: the learning organization

For the school as a living system, there is a creative tension between the personal, the technical and the organizational domains. As we have consistently argued, all three are important and should be utilized in the community in the service of learning, change and growth. When these are in healthy balance then new learning emerges – when one is too dominant then learning is stifled.

Assessment practices in schools are sites for real creative tensions. Our contention is that in recent years that creative tension has not been 'held' but has 'given in' to the dominance of high-stakes summative assessments, which we know 'scores an own goal' because the evidence suggests that this actually depresses motivation for learning (Harlen and Deakin Crick 2003a). Assessment practices must attend to the personal and the public, the formative and the summative and must enhance and enrich learning relationships.

Creative tensions: the learning system

In the schooling system a creative tension exists in the nature of the curriculum and the publicly valued knowledge, skills and competencies that form young people's entitlement. How young people encounter those skills and knowledge is crucially important to their motivation and progression – and the creative energy exists in the tension between a top down and a bottom-up approach. To what extent the system can prescribe knowledge, skills and competencies and to what extent the system can enable local solutions in relation to the curriculum is perhaps one of the most contested areas of education policy. To give in to either approach would not be satisfactory – the challenge is to allow novel solutions to emerge.

In a school system, particularly where schools find themselves in challenging situations, there is a tension between competition and collaboration, between being inward looking and partisan and outward looking and collaborative. Responsibility for innovation in teaching and learning is distributed widely among bodies with different terms of reference and remits – for example, higher education institutions, local authorities, non-government organizations and school partnerships. It is unclear how these potential partners may work together to co-generate knowledge and to disseminate and share that knowledge.

Meta themes

As we have worked through the ideas in this book, there have been some key themes that have emerged in different ways again and again. These, we believe, are characteristic of a schooling paradigm that enables personalized learning and distributed leadership and they are applicable to all individuals, to the organizations and to the system. We present them here as creative tensions, with their opposite poles.

Change and innovation	Tradition and continuity
Personal	Public
Taking responsibility for learning	Accepting external solutions
Power as relational	Power as control
Integration	Fragmentation
Engaged curriculum	Externally imposed curriculum
Creative professionalism	External control

Teaching and learning in 2020

During the time of writing this book the 2020 Review Group has published its findings (Gilbert 2006), espousing a national vision for the future of teaching and learning. At the heart of this vision is the idea of personalization which means focusing in a more structured way on each child's learning in order to enhance achievement, progress and participation. Gilbert and her committee argue that 'personalising learning has the potential to transform education' and that it is a matter of 'moral purpose and of social justice' (2006: 3–7).

Gilbert and her colleagues suggest that taking ownership of learning is at the heart of personalization and that there are three reciprocal core processes that schools can use to achieve this. These core processes map on to the first two stations of the learning journey:

- Pupil voice: establishing the habit of talking about learning and teaching and how to improve it *(the learning self)*.

- Learning how to learn: developing the skills and attitudes to become better learners *(the personal power to learn)*.

- Assessment for learning: coming to a shared understanding of learning goals and how to achieve them *(assessment as relational)*.

Informed professionalism – where school leaders take responsibility for their own professional learning and lead innovation and change in their communities – is the vehicle for achieving personalization. In our final section we will look at the implications of these ideas for leadership development – for the person who is leading, for the organization and for the system.

Leadership development: personal

Perhaps the single most significant personal development issue for leadership for personalization is what Senge (1990) calls 'personal mastery'. Organizations only learn through individuals who learn, and school leaders are 'primary culture bearers' in this respect, who set the tone for others and model their core values through 'who they are' and 'how they behave'. Senge (1990: 141) defines personal mastery as, 'The discipline of personal growth and learning. People with high levels of personal mastery are continually expanding their ability to create the results in life they truly seek. From their quest for continual learning comes the spirit of the learning organisation.'

He goes on to say that personal mastery is more than knowledge, skills and competencies and more than spiritual development – it is about approaching one's life as a creative work, living from a creative rather than a reactive viewpoint.

It is a discipline that needs to be integrated into the way one lives one's life and involves two processes:

- continually clarifying what really matters – our core values and vision
- continually learning how to see current reality more clearly.

In fact Senge says that lifelong generative learning emerges from the creative tension between our vision and values and our current reality – and learning organizations are not possible unless they have people at all levels who practise it. The personal power to learn is crucial for leaders – the dimensions of learning power can provide a language for articulating and structuring personal mastery.

Clarifying what really matters is personal. Core values and vision need to come from the inside – they are intrinsic and need to be recognized, articulated and mobilized. This form of creative work is a discipline that requires regular attention and the time and the space to attend to it. There is a growing movement of retreats, such as *Courage to teach* in the US and *Courage to be...the person you are in profession* in the UK – both inspired by the work of Parker Palmer – that create such spaces, where individuals can undertake this important inner work and call upon it in their outer, professional work.

Leadership development: organizational

The implications of these ideas for leadership development within a learning organization are that there should be the flexibility that enables the development of deep experience, deep learning and deep support for all adults in the system. A particularly important vehicle for this type of leadership development is coaching. Robertson (2005: 24) describes coaching as, 'A special, sometimes reciprocal relationship between (at least) two people who work together to set professional goals and achieve them. The term depicts a learning relationship where participants are open to new learning, engage together as professionals equally committed to facilitating each other's leadership learning development and well being (both cognitive and affective) and gain a greater understanding of professionalism and the work of professionals.'

Coaching, understood in this way, forms an important part of a learning journey for leaders and can be facilitated formally and informally within a learning culture in a school. Leaders at every stage of their career benefit from such learning relationships which model the sort of personalization of learning that we have been discussing throughout the book. A coaching relationship creates a space in which leaders can connect their learning to their lived experience in school in a way that formal training cannot, and thus can facilitate deep experience.

One of the challenges for education is how to connect theory and research evidence to practice – a coaching relationship which includes an academic specialist and a practitioner can be particularly fruitful in this respect since both parties benefit from the other's experience, and to some extent they have to learn each other's language. Leadership development for personalization requires leaders to be able to apply new educational ideas to novel situations – almost by definition there is no single formula that can be applied across the board. Equally, academics in education benefit from having their work 'earthed' in the real, messy world of schools.

At an organizational level, school leaders can develop a culture in which research evidence is both sought and created, and is seen to inform decision making. This requires time and attention to be given to such leadership development work. Planning in a research year prior to implementing a major new policy will not only create leadership development opportunities at many levels, but it will also ensure that when policies are implemented, they will have more solid foundations in evidence, rather than being simply pragmatic or faddish. They will be bespoke to the particular situation and community, and owned more deeply by those who have been responsible for researching and formulating them.

Such organizational learning requires the dynamic interaction of three stories: the story of the particular learning community; the story of the wider cultural and community tradition, including its research and evidence claims; and the story of the schooling system with its particular policy requirements. Each story is constituted by world views, values, traditions and resources which are relevant, and voices which call out to be heard in the leadership debates.

At the heart of the coaching relationship is dialogue, or learning conversations. Power is shared and in a relationship of trust, affirmation and challenge, both partners can take the risk of trying out new ideas, and formulating hypotheses and strategies in the light of the evidence before them. In this sort of context, the deep knowing that teachers have about learning can be brought forth, articulated and honoured – where, in more formal situations, it might remain hidden and unacknowledged – and critical analytical knowing can be 'clothed in experience'.

As well as coaching relationships, schools can organize small collaborative teams to address particular development issues. These may be shorter term and less deep than coaching relationships but they still facilitate the sort of development for leadership necessary for personalization. School INSET days can also be designed to enhance and support existing collaborative and coaching networks.

Leadership development: systems

The challenge for professional development for leadership in the system as a whole is profound. The ideas and practices we have described in this book require significant personal and professional knowledge, skills, values and attitudes that currently find a focus neither in initial teacher education, nor in continuing teacher education. Gilbert and colleagues (2006: 46) call for a 'system wide, schools-based reformed programme of continuing professional development that focuses initially on assessment for learning'. They suggest this should be characterized by:

- a focus on learning and teaching
- integration with daily practice
- iterative reflection on daily practice in the light of school's priorities
- teachers working in small teams.

Such a programme of professional learning cannot be delivered simply through training in which knowledge is presented to teachers at a single event. It requires a much deeper, coherent experience of professional learning that is distributed throughout the different spaces in the system – in school and out of school, in the academy and out of it, in the community and beyond. If it is achievable it would provide a loosely structured modus operandi for the sort of personalized, professional development for leadership which we have been advocating in this book. Aspiring leaders, at all stages, would be able to integrate their experience with their professional learning and avail themselves of the knowledge resources in the wider community. They would become strategically aware of themselves as learners, taking responsibility for their own learning journeys and co-generating knowledge within their communities, and they would be supported in doing so by the systems in which they operate.

At an educational systems level this produces a real challenge. There are many organizations who have a contribution to make to the co-generation of educational knowledge and know-how and thus to leadership development but there is often very little coordination or joined-up thinking between them, and they may hold conflicting values. For example, the reward systems in educational research institutions do not readily support academics working in practice in schools – and the reward systems in schools, especially those in challenging circumstances, focus on short-term increases in summative learning outcomes, rather than the longer-term culture change that we are describing in this book. Leadership development at a systems level requires an educational community where at least some people are multilingual – that is, they can understand and speak the languages of research, policy, practice and enterprise.

At the heart of leadership for personalized learning is the idea that leaders themselves lead in learning – and they need to be able to draw upon a range of resources and conversations in order to do that. Almost inevitably, such professional learning leads into an action research cycle, based on reflection, feedback, evidence and evaluation of previous actions and present experience. The learning of leaders is more public – their actions have an impact on a whole community – and it is important that the resources of the whole system (research, policy, practice and enterprise) are available to its leaders.

Within the higher-education community there is a movement towards public engagement. That is a way of working in research and teaching that reciprocally stimulates and supports the development of social and intellectual capital in business and the community. For schools and students (as part of the public) this requires what the Gilbert report describes as a 'strategy for systemic innovation'. That is a way of understanding, and a means of facilitating, the capture and dissemination of new knowledge and know-how that emerges from the different spaces in the system. This means a dynamic interaction between research, policy, practice and enterprise. In our view, there is a pressing need for regional and national collaboration in which the strengths of different stakeholders can be capitalized upon, in the service of an overall vision. For example, the research and development around learning power that we have described in this book is substantive enough to benefit from collaboration between schools, local authorities, different kinds of universities, businesses and non-government organizations such as think tanks and charities. When the traditional boundaries between these stakeholders are sufficiently 'plastic', and people can move easily between them, the core ideas and programmes can benefit from their combined energy – rather than, as is too often the case, be frustrated by apparently competing interests.

Conclusion

In this chapter we have been reminded of the deep changes associated with moving from a mechanical and industrial era into the information age of the twenty-first century. We have seen how the metaphor of an ecology or living system is useful in helping us understand some of these changes and how the development of an educational system that is capable of self-growth and renewal requires both personalized learning and the distribution of leadership at all levels of the system – individual, school, community and policy. Such an approach is fuelled by values of participation, social justice and human learning and growth.

To finish this chapter, we thought it worthwhile to consider, if pressed, how we would answer the question, 'What is the thing a leader needs most, to achieve these goals of personalizing learning and distributing leadership?' Is there an underlying virtue or quality without which none of the rest can happen, one which makes it all possible? There could, of course, be many answers. We believe that what is needed above all, in a leader of the kind we are depicting here, is a deep and genuine – indeed passionate – commitment to an inclusive, generous and coherent philosophy-in-action and the ethical courage that that implies. That is what supplies the driving energy that is fuelled by creative tension rather than confused by it, that is capable of deciding and directing without polarizing or alienating, that contains and fosters the courage to overcome great odds in a common cause and that builds the most precious commodity: confidence, in self and others, the hallmark of a living, growing, transformative learning community.

Bibliography

Alexander, R. (2004) 'Still no pedagogy? Principle, pragmatism and compliance in primary education', *Cambridge Journal of Education* 34 (1), 7–33

APA Work Group of the Board of Educational Affairs (1997) *Learner-centered psychological principles: A framework for school reform and redesign (revised edition)*, American Psychological Association, Washington DC

Arthur, J., Deakin Crick, R., Samuel, E., McGettrick, B. and Wilson, K. (2006) *Character Education: The Formation of Virtues and Dispositions in 16–19 Year Olds with particular reference to the religious and spiritual*, Christ Church Canterbury University, Canterbury

Assessment Reform Group (2002) *Testing, Motivation and Learning*, Assessment Reform Group, Cambridge

Barnes, D. (1975) *From communication to curriculum*, Harmondsworth, Penguin

Bell, D. and Ritchie, R. (1999) *Towards Effective Subject Leadership in the Primary School*, Open University Press, Buckingham

Bennett, N., Wise, C., Woods, P. and Harvey, J. (2003a) *Distributed Leadership – a review of the literature*, National College for School Leadership, Nottingham

Bennett, N., Newton, W., Wise, C., Woods, P. and Economou, A. (2003b) *The Role and Purpose of Middle Leaders in Schools*, National College for School Leadership, Nottingham

Bennis, W. (1989) *On Becoming a Leader*, Addison-Wesley Publishers, New York

Black, P., Mccormick, R., James, M. and Pedder, D. (2006) 'Assessment for learning and learning how to learn: a theoretical enquiry', *Assessment in Education: Policy and Practice,* 13

Bloom, B. (1956) *Taxonomy of Educational Objectives: the classification of educational goals, Handbook 1: cognitive domain*, Mackay, New York

Bond, T. (2004) *Ethical guidelines for researching counselling and psychotherapy*, Rugby: British Association for Counselling and Psychotherapy, Rugby

Bosher, M. and Hazlewood, P. (2005) *Nurturing Independent Thinkers: working with an alternative curriculum*, Network Educational Press, Stafford

Broadfoot, P. (1998) 'Records of achievement and the learning society: A tale of two discourses', *Assessment in Education,* 5, 447–477

Bryk, A. and Schneider, B. (2002) *Trust in Schools*, Russell Sage, New York

Bush, T. and Glover, D. (2003) *School Leadership: Concepts and Evidence*, National College for School Leadership, Nottingham

Chang-Wells, G. and Wells, G. (1993) 'Dynamics of discourse: Literacy and the construction of knowledge' in Forman, E., Minick, N. and Stone, A. (eds) *Contexts for learning: Sociocultural dynamics in children's development*, Oxford University Press, New York

Claxton, G. (2002) *Building Learning Power*, TLO, Bristol

Coffield, F., Moseley, D., Hall, E. and Ecclestone, K. (2004) *Should We Be Using Learning Styles?*, Learning and Skills Research Centre, London

Cole, M. and Engerstrom, Y. (1993) 'A cultural-historical approach to distributed cognition' in Salomon, G. (ed.), *Distributed cognitions: Psychological and educational considerations*, Cambridge University Press, New York

Darling-Hammond, L. (1990) 'Teacher Professionalism: why and how?' in Lieberman, E. (ed.), *Schools as Collaborative Cultures: Creating the Future now*, Falmer Press, New York

Darling-Hammond, L. (ed.) (1994) *Professional Development Schools: Schools for Developing a Profession*, Teachers College Press, New York

Day, C., Hall, C., Gammage, P. and Coles, M. (1993) *Leadership and Curriculum in the Primary School*, Paul Chapman, London

Day, C. and Saunders, L. (2006) *What being a teacher (really) means*, Forum, 48, 3

Deakin Crick, R. (2006) *Learning Power in Practice: a guide for teachers*, Paul Chapman, London

Deakin Crick, R., McCombs, B. and Hadden, A. (2007) 'The ecology of learning: factors contributing to learner centred classroom cultures', *Research Papers in Education*, 22

Deakin Crick, R., Small, T., Milner, N., Pollard, K., Jaros, M., Leo, E., Hearne, P., (2007) *Inquiring Minds: transforming potential through personalised learning*, RSA, London

Deakin Crick, R. and Wilson, K. (2005) 'Being a Learner: a Virtue for the 21st Century', *British Journal of Educational Studies*, Vol. 53, No 3, 359–374

De Frietas, S. and Yapp, C. (eds) (2005) *Personalizing Learning in the 21st Century*, Network Educational Press, Stafford

Demetriou, A. (2000) 'Organization and development of self-understanding and self-regulation: toward a general theory' in Boekarrts, M., Pintrich, P. and Zeidner, M. (eds), *Handbook Of Self-Regulation*, Academic Press, London

Department for Education and Skills (DfES) (2003) *Every Child Matters*, DfES, London

Department for Education and Skills (DfES) (2003) *Excellence and Enjoyment: a Strategy for Primary Schools*, DfES, London

Department for Education and Skills (DfES) (2004) *National Standard for Headteachers*, DfES, London

Department for Education and Skills (DfES) (2004) *The Children Act*, DfES, London

Department for Education and Skills (DfES) (2004) *Five Year Strategy for Children and Learners*, DfES, London

Department for Education and Skills (DfES) (2005) *Schools White Paper Higher Standards, Better Schools for All*, Chapter 4, Personalised Learning, DfES, London

Flavell, J. (1976) 'Metacognitive aspects of problem solving', *The Nature of Intelligence*, Lawrence Erlbaum Associates, Hillsdale NJ

Flutter, J. and Rudduck, J. (2004) *Consulting pupils: what's in it for schools?*, Routledge Falmer, London

Fukuyama, F. (1995) *Trust: The social virtues and the creation of prosperity*, Free Press, New York

Fullan, M. (1988) *What's worth fighting for in the principalship: Strategies for taking charge in the elementary school principalship*, Regional Laboratory for Educational Improvement of the Northeast & Islands, Ontario Public School Teachers' Federation

Fullan, M. (2003) *The Moral Imperative of School Leadership*, Sage Publications, London

Gardner, H. (1983) *Frames of Mind: The Theory of Multiple Intelligences*, Basic Books, New York

Ghaye, A. and Ghaye, K. (1998) *Teaching and Learning through Critical Reflective Practice*, David Fulton Publishers, London

Gilbert, C. (2006) *2020 vision: Report of teaching and learning in 2020 Review Group*, DfES, London

Goleman, D. (2002) *The New Leaders*, Little, Brown, London

Gronn, P. (2002a) 'Distributed Leadership as a unit of analysis', *Leadership Quarterly*, 13, 423–451

Gronn, P. (2002b) *The New Work of Educational Leaders*, Sage, London

Gunter, H. (2001) *Leaders and Leadership in Education*, Paul Chapman, London

Habermas, J. (1972) *Knowledge and Human Interest,* tr. Shapiro, J., Heinemann, London

Hadden, A., Park, J., Goodman, H. and Deakin Crick, R. (2005) 'Evaluating Emotional Literacy in schools: the development of the Schools Emotional Environment for Learning Survey', *Pastoral Care in Education*, 23, 4, 5–16

Hallinger, P., Leithwood, K. and Murphy, J. (1993) *Cognitive perspectives on educational leadership*, Teachers College Press, New York

Hargreaves, A. (2003) *Teaching in the Knowledge Economy: education in the age of insecurity*, Open University Press, Maidenhead

Hargreaves, D. (2004) *Personalising Learning: next steps in working laterally*, Specialist Schools Trust, London

Harlen, W. and Deakin Crick, R. (2003a) *A systematic review of the impact of summative assessment and testing on pupils' motivation for learning*, Evidence for Policy and Practice Co-ordinating Centre, Department for Education and Skills, London

Harlen, W. and Deakin Crick, R. (2003b) 'Testing and motivation for learning', *Assessment in Education*, 10

Harris, A. (2004) 'Distributed Leadership and School Improvement: Leading or Misleading?', *Educational, Management, Administration and Leadership*, 32 (1), 11–24

Harris, A. and Lambert, L. (2003) *Building Leadership Capacity for School Improvement*, Open University Press, Buckingham

Hart, T. (2001) *From information to transformation: Education for the evolution of consciousness*, Peter Lang, New York

Hartle, F. and Thomas, K. (2003) *Growing Tomorrow's Leaders: the challenge*, National College for School Leadership, Nottingham

Haste, H. (2001) 'Ambiguity, autonomy and agency' in Rychen, D. and Salganik, L. (eds), *Definition and Selection of Competencies; Theoretical and Conceptual Foundations,* OECD, Hogreffe and Huber, Seattle

Hauenstein, A. (1998) *A Conceptual Framework for Educational Objectives: a holistic approach to traditional taxonomies*, University Press of America, Lanham MD

Hobby, R. (2001) *Teacher effectiveness and leadership: a framework for lifelong learning*, Primary Leadership Paper 3 (June) (11–12), National Association of Head Teachers

Holland, J. (1998) *From chaos to order*, Oxford, Oxford University Press

Hopkins, D. and Jackson, D. (2003) *Networked Learning Communities – Capacity Building, Networking and Leadership for Learning*, National College for School Leadership, Nottingham

Howe, A., Davies, D. and Ritchie, R. (2001) *Design and Technology for the Future: Creativity, Culture and Citizenship*, David Fulton Publishers, London

James, M. and Pollard, A. (2006) *Improving Teaching and Learning in Schools*, TLRP, ESRC

Jackson, D. (2002a) *Distributed Leadership – Spaces Between the Pebbles in the Jar (a think piece)*, National College for School Leadership, Nottingham

Jackson, D. (2002b) *Networked Learning Communities: the Journey So Far*, National College for School Leadership, Nottingham

Jaros, M. and Deakin Crick, R. (2006) 'Personalised learning in the post mechanical age', *Journal of Curriculum Studies*, 38

John-Steiner, V., Panofsky, C. and Smith, L. (1994) *Socio-cultural approaches to language and literacy: An interactionist perspective*, Cambridge University Press, New York

Leadbeater, C. (2005) *The Shape of Things to Come: personalised learning through collaboration*, DfES, London

Leithwood, K. (1994) 'Leadership for school restructuring', *Educational Administration Quarterly*, 30 (4), 498–518

Leithwood, K., Jantzi, D. and Steinbach, R. (1999) *Changing Leadership for Changing Times*, Open University Press, Buckingham

Leo, E., Deakin Crick R., Yu, G. and Hearne P. (2007) 'Underachievement and learning power', *forthcoming*

MacBeath, J. and McGlynn, A. (2002) *Self Evaluation: What's in it for Schools?*, Routledge/Falmer, London

MacBeath, J., Oduro, G. K. T. and Waterhouse, J. (2004) *Distributed Leadership in Action: A study of current practice in schools* [full report available in the CD-ROM in the NCSL's boxed set, 'Distributed Leadership'], NCSL, Nottingham

McCombs, B. and Whisler, J. (1997) *The Learner Centered Classroom and School: Strategies for Increasing Student Motivation and Achievement*, San Francisco, Jossey Bass

McCombs, B. (1997) *Self-Assessment and Reflection: Tools for Promoting Teacher Changes toward Learner-Centered Practices*, University of Denver Research Institute for Human Motivation and Development, Denver

McCombs, B. and Miller, M. (2006) *Learner-centered classroom practices and assessments*, Thousand Oaks CA, Corwin Press

Milner, N. (2006) *Learning by accident: a report of a personalised learning project for disengaged young learners*, Bristol ViTaL Partnerships

Mosely, D., Baumfield, V., Elliot, J., Gregson, M., Higgins, S., Miller, J. and Newton, D. (2005) *Frameworks for Thinking: A Handbook for Teaching and Learning*, Cambridge University Press, Cambridge

Murphy, J., and Beck G. (1993) *Understanding the Principalship: Metaphorical Themes 1920s – 1990s*, Teachers College Press, New York

NACCCE/DfEE (1999) *All Our Futures: Creativity, Culture and Education*, DfEE, London

NAHT (2001*) Primary Leadership Paper 3: Teacher Effectiveness and Leadership*, National Association of Headteachers, London

NCSL (2004a) *Distributed Leadership* (Boxed set of materials), National College for School Leadership, Nottingham

NCSL (2004b) *Learning-centred Leadership Pack*, National College for School Leadership, Nottingham

NCSL (2005a) *Leading Personalised Learning in Schools: Helping individuals grow*, NCSL, Nottingham

NCSL (2005b) *Personalised Learning: Tailoring learning solutions for every pupil*, A Special LDR Supplement, NCSL, Nottingham

Ofsted (1999) *Handbook for Inspecting Primary and Nursery Schools with Guidance on Self-evaluation*, Ofsted Publications Centre, London

Ofsted (2003) *Leadership and Management: What inspection tells us*, Ofsted, London

Ofsted (2005a) *A New Relationship with Schools: Improving Performance through School Self-evaluation*, Ofsted, London

Ofsted (2006) *HMCI speech to Leeds Conference*, Ofsted, London

Ofsted (2007) *Inspection Report: Waycroft School*, Ofsted, London

O'Sullivan, E. (2003) 'Bringing a perspective of transformative learning to globalised consumption', *International Journal of Consumer Studies, 27, 326–330*

Ollerenshaw, C. and Ritchie, R. (1997) Primary Science: Making it Work (2nd edn), David Fulton Publishers, London

Palmer, P. (1983) *To know as we are known: a spirituality of education*, Harper & Row, San Francisco

Palmer, P. (1998) *The courage to teach*, Jossey-Bass, San Francisco

Palmer, P. (2000) *Let your life speak: Listening for the voice of vocation*, Jossey-Bass, San Francisco

Palmer, P. (2004) *A hidden wholeness; the journey toward an undivided life*, Jossey-Bass, San Francisco

Pollard, A. and James, M. (eds) (2004) *Personalised Learning: A Commentary By The Teaching And Learning Research Programme*, ESRC TLRP, Cambridge

Powell, G., Chambers, M. and Baxter, G. (2001) *Pathways to coaching: a guide for team leaders*, TLO Ltd, Bristol

Putnam, R. (2000) *Bowling alone: The collapse and revival of American community*, Simon & Schuster, New York

Ritchie, R. (2001) *Design and Technology: a process for learning (2nd edn)*, David Fulton Publishers, London

Ritchie, R. (2002) 'School improvement in the context of a primary school in special measures', *Journal of Teacher Development*, Vol. 6, No 3, 329–346

Ritchie, R. (2004) *Leadership Development and Succession Planning: Final Report*, SWAC/UWE, Bristol

Ritchie, R. (2006) *The Bristol Leaders of Learning Project (BRiLL)*, University of West of England, Bristol

Ritchie, R. (2007a) 'Degrees of Distribution: Towards an understanding of variations in the nature of distributed leadership in schools' (with Woods, P.), *School Leadership and Management*, forthcoming

Ritchie, R. (2007b) 'School self-evaluation' in Kushner, S. and Norris, N. (eds), *Dilemmas of Engagement: Evaluation Development Under New Public Management and the New Politics*, Elsevier, New York

Ritchie, R. and Ikin, J. (2000) *Telling Tales of School Improvement*, National Primary Trust, Birmingham

Robertson, J. (2005) *Coaching Leadership: Building Educational Leadership Capacity through Coaching Partnerships*, NZCER Press, Wellington

Rogoff, B. (1994) 'Developing understanding of the idea of communities of learners', *Mind, Culture and Activity*, 1, 209–229

Rogers, C. (1994) *Freedom to learn*, Merrill, Ohio

Rudduck, J. and Flutter, J. (2004) *How to improve your school: Giving pupils a voice*, Continuum, London

Salovey, P. and Mayer, J. (1990) 'Emotional intelligence', *Imagination, Cognition and Personality*, 9, 185–211

Schon, D. (1983) *The reflective practitioner: How professionals think in action*, Temple Smith, London

Schluter, M. (2003) *Building a relational society new priorities for public policy*, Relationships Foundation, Cambridge

Senge, P. (1990*) The Fifth Discipline*, Doubleday, New York

Senge, P., Scharmer, C. O., Jaworski, J. and Flowers, B. (2004) *Presence: Human purpose and the field of the future*, Nicholas Brearley Publishing, Cambridge, Mass

Sergiovanni, T. J. (2001) *Leadership: What's in it for schools?*, Routledge Falmer, London

Small, T. and Burn, M. (2006) *The Learning Engineers: Bridging values and learning*, Report No 2, Bristol ViTaL Partnerships

Southworth, G. (2004) 'How Leaders influence what happens in Classrooms' in *Learning-centred Leadership Pack*, NCSL, Nottingham

Spillane, J., Diamond, J. and Jita, L. (2003) 'Leading instruction: The distribution of leadership for instruction', *Journal of Curriculum Studies*, 35

Temple, S. (2002) 'Functional fluency for educational transactional analysts', *Zeitschrift fur Transaktionasanalyse, 4*

Temple, S. (2004) 'Building self-awareness', *Emotional Literacy Update*, Antidote, London

Tobin, K. (1987) 'The Role of Wait Time in Higher Cognitive Level Learning', *Review of Educational Research*, 57, 69–95

Tutu, D. (2000) *No Futures without Forgiveness,* Bantam Doubleday Dell Publishing Group Inc., London

Vygotsky, L. (1978) *Mind in society: The development of higher psychological processes*, Harvard University Press, Cambridge, Mass

West-Burnham, J. (1996) 'Quality and the Primary School Curriculum' in O'Neill, J. and Kitson, N. (eds) (1996) *Effective Curriculum Management: co-ordinating learning in the primary school*, Routledge, London

West-Burnham, J. (2004) *Leadership Development and Personal Effectiveness Thinkpiece*, National College for School Leadership, Nottingham

West-Burnham, J. (2005) ' Leadership for Personalizing Learning' in De Frietas, S. and

Yapp, C. (eds) *Personalizing Learning in the 21st Century*, Network Educational Press, Stafford

West-Burnham, J. and Coates, M. (2005) *Personalizing Learning: Transforming education for every child*, Network Educational Press, Stafford

Wheatley, M. (1999) *Leadership and the New Science*, Berrett-Koehler, US

White, J. (2004) *Howard Gardner: the myth of Multiple Intelligences*, Institute of Education, London (Lecture, 17 November)

Whitehead, J. (1989) 'How do we improve research-based professionalism in education?', *British Educational Research Journal*, 15 (1), 3–15

Williams, S. (2007) *Enabling Transformative Change in a 'salugenic' place* (working title), PhD Thesis, University of Bristol

Winter, R. (1989) *Learning from Experience*, The Falmer Press, Lewes

Woods, P.A. (2004) 'Democratic Leadership: Drawing distinctions with distributed leadership', *International Journal of Leadership in Education: Theory and Practice*, 7 (1), 3–26

Woods, P., Bennett, N., Wise, C. and Harvey, J. (2004) 'Variabilities and Dualities in understanding distributed leadership: findings from a systematic literature review', *Educational, Management, Administration and Leadership*, 32 (4), 439–457

Woods, R. (2002) *Enchanted Headteachers: Sustainability in primary school headship*, National College for School Leadership, Nottingham

Woods, P. (2005) *Democratic Leadership in Education*, Paul Chapman Publishing, London

Wright, A. (2000) *Spirituality and Education*, Routledge Falmer, London

Zimmerman, B. (2000) 'Attaining Self-Regulation' in Boekarrts, M., Pintrich, P. and Zeidner, M. (eds) *Handbook of Self-Regulation*, Academic Press, London

Index